Clarissa and the Countryman

Sally Forth

Also by Clarissa Dickson Wright:

The Haggis: a Little History
Food
Hieland Foodie: A Scottish Culinary Voyage with Clarissa

with Jennifer Paterson
Two Fat Ladies
Two Fat Ladies Ride Again
Two Fat Ladies: Full Throttle
Two Fat Ladies: Obsessions

Contents

HONDA

INTRODUCTION

In our first television series in the autumn of 2000 we illustrated the indivisible thread that links farming, country sports and conservation. The aim of the second series, more than a year on, was to explore this theme further. We little knew, as we planned the programmes in January 2001, that the outbreak of foot and mouth disease would result in the slaughter of four and a half million animals, devastate rural businesses across the country, and lead to the cancellation of all sporting, equine and agricultural events. It has provided a chilling foretaste of our present government's vision for rural Britain.

In writing this book, we wanted to share our belief that country sports are an essential part of the countryside and its way of life. We celebrate the urban sportsman who keeps in touch with his rural background through his terriers and ferrets. We visit some of the industries that would be affected should our Labour Government succeed in banning country sports and admire the skills of the many craftsmen whose livelihoods are under threat. We show how country sports have shaped our landscape and continue to play an essential role in creating wildlife habitats. And, at a time when farming is also under threat, we touch on some of the opportunities for diversification, which has become so essential to farmers.

Our thanks go out again to all the contributors who selflessly gave of their time and energy in the most depressing of times and whose enthusiasm for the countryside, its sports and industries kept us going when all seemed dark and impossible. Our thanks to Jane Root, Controller of BBC2 for recommissioning the series and to Colin Cameron, Head of Network Programmes at the BBC, for his support and encouragement and to all who have worked with us. Once again, against endless impediments, to all at Headline for producing a second lovely book. Finally, thanks to all of you who buy the book and watch the programmes and let us know that what we do finds favour.

Clarissa Dickson Wright Johnny Scott

CHAPTER ONE

For the Love of a Tyke

Always remember your terriers,
Protect them from wet and from cold,
For the love of a tyke for its master
Can never be measured in gold.

D. P. Todd

J Goodness knows how old the terrier is as a breed. The sheer range of shapes, sizes, colours and coats developed over many centuries is an indication of their antiquity. Wild dogs were the first animal that prehistoric man domesticated and originally they would have been bred for size to hunt game in the open. At some point, man the hunter recognised the need for a small, fearless dog to bolt game from dense cover and vermin from below ground. The little creature that evolved was the ancestor of today's terrier. Whatever their breed, all terriers have, to a greater or lesser degree, the same characteristics, which are both endearing and utterly maddening: pluck, intelligence, loyalty and bobberiness – that quality of obstreperous, quarrelsome ebullience. All of them adhere to the terrier's maxim: if it moves, bark at it; if it doesn't, cock your leg on it.

What did they look like, those ancestors of the terrier of today? A wire-haired dachsund, probably. As early as c.1430 BC, a dog not dissimilar to a dachsie could be seen on top of a monument keeping Tuthmosis III, the Napoleon of Egypt, company. The Greeks, the first sporting gentlemen farmers and keen hound men, must have had them and passed the priceless canine legacy on to the Romans – after all, the name terrier comes from *terra*, the Latin for earth – along with their love of coursing. Your sporting Celt, not unlike terriers themselves for obstreperousness, hunted deer for the larder and fox and hare for sport with their basset-like Silusian hounds, and would surely have had terriers. Without terriers for inspiration, would the early Briton, that dreamy herdsman, have thought to breed his famous rough-coated Agassean, the ancestor of the Welsh hound? Or St Hubert, the patron saint of hunting, his great, black, scenting hound of the Ardennes? I see them strutting with monstrous self-importance through the courtyards of our Norman conquerors, shrieking with fury and frustration when the black and tan Talbots, the mottled Gascons and small beagly Brachets were all packed together to hunt the forest deer and they were left in kennels. They would have come into their own for fox, badger and particularly otter work.

In the days when the fish in our rivers and stew ponds were as valuable as the deer in the forests, otters were rightly considered destructive vermin. Otter hunting and the use of terriers to bolt them from their holts was essential to their control and the protection of inland fisheries. Indeed, otter hunting was so important that a King's Otter Hunter, Roger Follo, was appointed by Henry II in 1175. Royal patronage was bestowed both on the hounds and on the hardy, rough-coated, leggy terriers that ran with the pack, and continued through successive reigns for five hundred years.

The first mention of terriers is in that much reprinted definitive tome on hunting, Dame Juliana Berners' *Boke of St Albans* (1486). 'Thyse be the names of houndes,' the old girl wrote laboriously. 'First there is A greyhoun; A Bastard; A Mongrel; A Mastif; A Lemor; A Spanyel; Raches; Kenettys; Teroures.' A Bastard was a lurcher, and a Lemor a bloodhound. Raches were foxhounds. Kennettys were smaller hounds. These and the Teroures made up the sort of bobbery pack that was invariably part of every gentleman's establishment.

George Turberville, one of the first great sporting authors, wrote about them in *The Noble Art* (1576), and at much the same time a terrier appears in art. Brueghel the Elder's 'Winter Landscape' depicts a man carrying a dead fox over his shoulder. He is obviously conforming strictly to MFHA Rule No 18: 'All carcasses of dead foxes, whether caught by hounds or dug out, should be picked up and disposed of.' Around him, as he plods along with his long pole, are his lurcher, his greyhound, his bloodhound and, stotting along like a flyweight boxer and claiming all the credit, his teroure.

Until as recently as the early nineteenth century, terriers were of three basic types. One, similar to the old-fashioned Welsh terrier, was long-legged, rough-coated and probably black and tan; another, that seems to have evolved in the south, was short-legged and smooth-coated; and the third was a wire-coated type known loosely as the Scotch terrier, which covered all those that are now standardised as Cairns, Skyes, white West Highlands – a dog that bears no resemblance to those that Colonel Malcolm of Poltalloch hunted otters with in Argyllshire – and Border terriers (the original Dandie Dinmonts as opposed to those long-haired jobs).

The increased mobility that followed the Agricultural and Industrial Revolutions of the eighteenth and nineteenth centuries brought great improvements in all livestock breeding as the best in one area were selected to improve those in another. This was the glorious age when hunting was developed along the lines we know it today and a new kind of foxhound was required to meet the challenge of the altered countryside. Accessibility meant that bloodlines could be exchanged between packs, and great names like Hugo Meynell of Quorndon and Peter Beckford were among the many that have become part of history. The same was true of terriers. Judicious crossing to produce types best suited to a particular area or need, such as the Yorkshire terrier, bred specifically to control rats in the mills, gradually created the standardisation of the many different breeds we know today.

My father had two ambitions in life: one was to breed the perfect weight-carrying hunter; the other was to breed what he considered the perfect working terrier. He aimed for a wire-coated terrier, between 11 and 12 inches at the shoulder and 11–12 pounds in weight, with dead straight forelegs and powerful hindquarters. It should be broad-headed with high-set lugs and a square muzzle, and predominantly white-coloured with black or tan points around the eyes or body. Too much colour would have made them less easy to see on rabbiting days or on a dig. The ancestor of all my father's terriers was Tiger, a Sealyham cross that he acquired from Jack Champion of the famous hunting dynasty when Jack came to the Old Surrey and Burstow as Huntsman in 1947. This was the old-fashioned Sealyham, the type developed for otter hunting by the breed's founder, that great Welsh sportsman Captain Edwardes of Sealyham in Pembrokeshire, and bearing no resemblance, except in its long-haired, wiry, waterproof coat, to the ridiculous short-coupled toy of show ring and drawing room.

Tiger, an immensely hardy dog combining stamina, courage and common sense, and standing 14 inches at the shoulder, was crossed with Tweedle, a 10-inch smooth-coated bitch from Frank Chilman, who had been my grandfather's keeper at Tremaynes and Danehurst before the war. Tweedle was of the type incorrectly called a fox terrier or, worse, a Jack Russell. For pedants such as myself, no such dog exists. The Reverend J. Russell had a certain type of working terrier, predominantly white, leggy and rough-coated. He never standardised his terriers into a breed but every terrier with white markings, regardless of size or coat, seems to be called a Jack Russell. Tweedle was simply a smooth-coated working terrier, and needle sharp with it. With these two, my father had enormous fun rabbiting in the immediate post-war years.

My earliest childhood memories are of hearing, from the nursery wing, what seemed to be a never- ending dog fight which reverberated back and forth through the rest of the house as Tiger and Tweedle and their offspring flew to investigate some unfamiliar sound, almost certainly imperceptible to the human ear. It is a noise that has been familiar to me all my life and was no doubt the first sound that my own children learnt to recognise.

From Tiger and Tweedle I had my first lessons in treating animals with respect and the beginnings of an understanding of a dog's perspective. When I was five years old, one of those red-letter days occurred when my mother and sister were away. It was the nanny's afternoon off and I had my father all to myself. To find something to occupy us both, he decided to trim back a length of hedge that ran up to a spinney. I was helping in my ineffectual way, dragging the cut hedging aside. It was hot, and quite early in the proceedings my father took off his coat and laid it on the ground. Tiger, ignoring the other terriers squabbling around a rabbit hole, immediately came and sat on it. Later in the afternoon, when the midges were becoming unbearable and it was time to go home, my father sent me back up the hedge line to get his coat. For some reason I had an overwhelming desire to put it on and come back wearing it. As I approached the place where the coat lay, I saw that Tiger was still *in situ*. Normally he and I got on quite well considering that I was a threat to his master's affections. He treated me with amicable contempt and I only took a liberty with his tail once. Now he greeted me with bared fangs and a deep, sinister growl. This was very awkward. Personal vanity and a desperate desire to please necessitated my reappearing suitably clad. Tiger, on the other hand, as the crescendo of snarls indicated, was not parting with the coat to anyone other than its owner. Not even a close relation.

My father had an extraordinary way with animals. Until he became too old to cope with more than one, he never had fewer than four terriers at any time, and they all adored him. They were a picture of woeful desolation when he went on his monthly visit to the farms in Northumberland, leaving them behind. Otherwise they went everywhere with him, as familiar a sight following the hunters on morning exercise as they were in the village shop, the pub, the belfry of our church on Sunday mornings when he rang with the bellringers, and the cricket pitch when he was fielding. At night, they twitched and whimpered on their dream hunts in cardboard boxes filled with old shooting stockings or cast-off jerseys in his dressing room, with the oldest one sleeping on the foot of his bed.

The feeling was reciprocated and there was a period when my father, the least neurotic of men, convinced himself that vivisectionists, and dog thieves in their employ, were conspiring to steal one or all of his cherished companions when on one of their nefarious visits to the village. It never dawned on him that no one, vivisectionist or not, would have been able to get near one of his terriers without instantly and painfully regretting it. Much thought was devoted to means of outwitting this new evil stalking the land. Finally, he heard of an organisation that, according to him, had reached an agreement with vivisectionists. Dogs with a positive proof of identification would be returned to their owners or the police. 'How do you achieve that?' I asked him, knowing that he would never put a collar on a terrier for fear of them getting hooked up underground. 'You have your National Insurance number tattooed on the inside of their thigh,' he told me succinctly, with the air of a man who has successfully solved an insuperable problem and discovered, for the first time, that he possessed such a thing as a National Insurance number.

Tattooing as a means of dog registration was very much in its infancy and I don't suppose anyone had attempted to do it on half a dozen terriers like my father's. It was a shambles. The tack room, in which this delicate operation was undertaken, was covered in ink. The tattooist, inveigled from the nearby town, was severely bitten and only mollified with such quantities of whisky that he had to be driven home, bandaged and paralytic. Six outraged terriers stalked about for days, stiff-legged, and bore tattoos that were completely illegible for the rest of their lives. Worse, the William Hickey column of the *Daily Express* found out about it and wrote a piece which started, 'Eccentric baronet, Sir Walter Scott, not content with devoting his life to the mounted pursuit of vermin, has invented a new sport. He tattoos his dogs...'

Much to the despair of my mother, my father firmly believed that too much discipline inhibited natural development. As far as he was concerned, the dogs could do absolutely no wrong. Their worst excesses were lovingly related, and date of entry and performance below ground religiously recorded. Each terrier had a name beginning with T and over the years we had, between us, Tiger, Tweedle, Tory, Tosh, Toggle, Tufton, Tiger again, Trouble, Trooper, Tink, Temper, Tantrum, Terror and the present incumbent, Tug.

My father had the good fortune to die in his own bed, after a decent dinner and his usual soporific, at the end of a full and active life devoted to the countryside he loved. He shared his declining years with the aptly named Terror, a dog notorious for never being able to resist a grandchild's chubby leg, a habit which excused them wearing gumboots in the house. On the unhappy day, two ambulance men arrived to remove the mortal remains and were directed to his dressing room. Shortly afterwards a scream of pain and muttered oaths were heard from above. One ambulance man was discovered clutching his ankle, perched on top of my father. The other, in a corner, was protecting himself with the stretcher. From beneath the bed, Terror was paying my father the final compliment. How he would have loved it.

I was given my first terrier when I was six. The second of the Tigers, he had been bought from Frank Chilman to correct size and coat in my father's breeding programme and, using all the wiles of a determined child, I made the pup mine. With him I explored the countryside and did all the things a young boy does with a terrier – you see and learn a thousand things that would otherwise pass unnoticed. We hunted rats round the farm buildings, ferreted together and chased squirrels, and I glowed with pride when Roy Goddard, the Southdown's Huntsman, let me enter him to a fox that had been run to ground one lovely frosty day at the end of the season, when Tiger was two. Terriers behave below ground in the same way as they do above: they bark. With luck their barking bolts the fox through the rear entrance. Roy's 'You've got a good 'un there, boy,' when the fox finally bolted, is with me yet.

Tiger was my closest friend and I told him all my secrets. We were inseparable during the holidays and parting from him at the beginning of each term had much to do with my loathing school. There is a portrait in pastel of us both, done by Raymond Piper when I was sixteen. Raymond drew me seated in an armchair with the old dog curled up asleep in the crook of my arm. It encapsulates the relationship between a boy and his terrier which I have so often seen with my son Sam and his first dog Temper. Every boy should have a terrier. Indeed, their loyalty and *joie de vivre* make them an ideal pet for any age.

To anyone living on a farm, rats are an ongoing problem, but most people in urban areas are blissfully unaware that they are almost never less than two yards away from a rat. This is the universally hated brown rat that moved westwards in hordes from the more temperate areas of Siberia, which was their home, invading Russia and Norway in the late 1720s. It arrived in England towards the end of George I's reign and was at that time known as the Hanoverian rat. Loyal Jacobites used to drink a toast to 'The King over the sea and the expulsion of the Hanoverian rat'. Brown rats breed in their first year and can produce up to seven litters of between ten and twenty young. In no time the brown rat had virtually wiped out the much nicer but still pretty revolting old English black rat. Rats cause an incredible amount of damage – it must run into tens of millions of pounds annually – and their fleas spread a variety of diseases that are positively medieval in their horridness. I should know. I once had jaundice which, my doctor told me, just as the fever was reaching its peak, I had probably caught from eating fruit that rats had piddled on. Thereafter, my nightmares were populated by gigantic, leg-cocking rats.

Industrialisation caused great shifts in population as villages and towns such as Birmingham, Liverpool, Manchester, Newcastle and Glasgow became cities almost overnight. Immigrants flooded in from Ireland and, with continued advances in agriculture, from rural areas across Britain. The exodus from village to town that began with the Agricultural and Industrial Revolutions has been particularly dramatic this century. In the fifty years since the

Second World War, the agricultural workforce has been reduced by something approaching 70 per cent. Like their predecessors, these refugees from the countryside brought with them a tangible connection between their strange new existence and their rural background. Every town and city is home to an incredible number of ferrets, lurchers, gundogs and the traditional working man's companion, terriers.

Johnny with Tiger, by Raymond Piper

There is a thriving network of working terrier clubs in both town and country. As well as the useful and legal activity of working terriers to their natural quarry, they provide an opportunity for people with a common interest to meet regularly. The Merseyside Working Terrier and Lurcher Club (MWTLC) is a classic example. It was started in 1980 by Dave Moorcroft, the current chairman, the Goulden brothers (Billy, Steven and John) and Peter Smith, and began life as a rescue organisation for abandoned terriers and lurchers in Liverpool. In due course they arranged sporting outings to quarry pack meets, particularly fell packs, beagles and mink hounds with whom they could participate on foot, and soon attracted invitations from the farming community to help with vermin control.

Mark Roberts did sterling work as chairman for eight years, and in 1995 it occurred to Kevin Nolan, the club secretary, that the happy days spent out of Liverpool, the ferreting, ratting and camaraderie of the hunting field, the knowledge of field craft and of his national heritage had only become available to him through his membership of the club. We all have a responsibility to 'pass it on' and the increased threat of political interference with a way of life to which he and his members were passionately attached led Kevin to suggest starting a junior membership. Its purpose was to introduce local children to an alternative way of life before it disappeared. Now, in addition to its regular membership, the club has an average of thirty juniors aged between ten and sixteen, all of whom wear the dark green club teeshirt with immense pride.

The Merseyside boys are instructed in the training and welfare of terriers and, when they are considered responsible, helped to acquire one. They provide an invaluable service, ratting in areas where the council is unable to use poison. With the help of local farmers and landowners for whom the club controls vermin they are taught the intricacies of ferreting and learn the importance of respecting property and livestock, including that essential of the country, shutting gates. They go on trips to game fairs and country shows, on days out with neighbouring foxhound packs, and to coursing meetings such as the nearby Waterloo Cup. There are clay pigeon days to introduce the boys to gun safety and the basics of handling a shotgun, and the fascinating falconry demonstrations given by Terry Large.

Going ratting

Lee Haslam, whom we had met at the 2000 Waterloo Cup, put it very neatly in his letter inviting us down for a couple of days' ratting. 'The kids we cater for are from deprived inner-city areas where crime and drugs figure most. So we feel that if we can give our juniors the right advice and opportunities, they may avoid crime. If they are in the field with ferret and dog, they're not in harm's way, i.e. car crime, vandalism, etc.'

Lee's invitation had generously included Tug, which was pretty big-hearted of him, and I can only assume that Tug's reputation hadn't reached Liverpool. I bought Tug off a chap who does fox control up near Braemar. Tug's mother was a bitch from the David Davies and his father came from the College Valley. In the parlance he was 'right way bred', but somewhere in his genealogy there had been an outcross to a white English bull terrier and Tug inherited many of this ancestor's characteristics. In fact he looks not unlike one, reduced to about a third of the size. From behind, he has massively muscled hindquarters and the alligator gait unique to a bull terrier, and is completely bone-headed. He has an over-exaggerated sense of territory and cocks his leg on anything or anyone who stands still long enough for him to take aim. Christmas is a bad time for Tug, with all those parcels and guests' suitcases that have to be familiarised. He never quite enters into the Yuletide spirit until each one has got its little yellow droplet. Any journey with him is a torment; the sight of another dog drives him insane and it is completely out of the question to leave him in a car unattended. Having said all that, I love him dearly. He has a marvellous nose and can scent rats underground well away from their holes. The Sunday before we left I had a magical day ratting with him, and the euphoria of this and Clarrie's entreaties on his behalf persuaded me, if with extreme misgivings, to allow him to come. The extraordinary thing is that his behaviour was impeccable throughout our trip.

Huyton, where Lee lives on the outskirts of Liverpool, is an area of high unemployment

Liverpool skyline

and reflects the despair of that situation. Street after street of grim post-war council houses, many of them boarded up, are set against a backdrop of high-rise flats. Periodically you come across a house which, despite its surroundings, displays all the pride of ownership, with a pristine front garden, immaculate window boxes and gleaming paintwork. I would have recognised one of these as Lee and Eileen's home even if there hadn't been a group of boys standing outside it, dressed in old Barbours and their club teeshirts, with a terrier apiece.

These, under the watchful eye of Dave Moorcroft, were some of the Merseyside boys. The club reckons that six is a manageable number of lads and terriers on a field trip. This outing's lucky selection were three sixteen-year-olds, Tully, Snudge and Gary, with what proved to be a really topping Lakeland cross Border bitch called Jess, a some way bred bitch that I thought a bit leggy, and a perfect example of a black Fell bitch called Tick. Curtis and Roz, aged fourteen and thirteen respectively, had a rough-coated Sealyham cross dog, Fawn, and a little smooth-haired black and white bitch called Tina, and last, but not least, was Conker, ten years old and hanging on to Dave's chocolate-coloured Patterdale Clay as if his life depended on it. With Dave carrying the strimmer engine and hosepipe for smoking out the rats, Lee carrying the fishing net for catching them when they broke cover and made off downstream, and Clarissa clutching her rat-splatting shillelagh, we set off to the meet, on the banks of the river Alt, two streets away.

The Alt rises in Huyton and its treatment over the few miles before it escapes into the sea between Crosby and Formby has earned it the reputation of being the most polluted river in Europe. Where we were, it is perhaps four feet wide and crammed with every conceivable sort of household waste. It is a dumping ground for old baths, broken lavatories and bits and pieces of unwanted furniture. Every few yards a shopping trolley protrudes from the scummy water. 'This is the place to dump the murder weapon,' I said to myself. 'No one in their right mind would dream of going in to look for it.' The banks, softened with rotting food, are covered in filth and riddled with rat holes. The nests of those we were to dig out during the course of the day were lined, not with hay and leaves like those in the country, but with greasy bits of plastic, scraps of rotting fabric, old sticking plasters and yes, there were a few of those too.

The boys slipped into a well-practised routine, perfected on previous outings along the length of the Alt, on railway embankments and down among the docks. A couple of them went up and downstream to look for droppings and pad marks along the water's edge. The rest of us positioned ourselves at places where the rats were likely to bolt. Dave connected the hose and started the strimmer. Lee got ready with the net, Clarissa brandished her shillelagh and seven terriers gripped by the scruff of the neck strained forward as the exhaust fumes were revved into the first hole.

When the rats bolt they are incredibly fast. They come out of their holes like champagne

Tug watching a rat's bolt hole

corks. The terriers, anticipating them, are equally quick, and any that take to the water are pursued by Lee, who is a dab hand with the net. It was the most incredible fun, slipping and sliding along the banks of the Alt, clambering over the refuse and desperately trying to keep clear of the water. Even in their excitement, the terriers showed a remarkable sense of self-preservation, using the shopping trolleys as a means of crossing from bank to bank. They are artists at their work, and few rats got by them.

We moved to different beats along the Alt on a number of occasions during the day. Sometimes we went on foot and sometimes we all piled in and out of the cars, but we were always in areas of high-density housing. What really astonished me was that not one of the people who passed us saw anything the least unusual about four adults, six lads of different ages and seven assorted terriers bolting rats with a strimmer engine.

We had to hose Tug down that night and rub him over with dock leaves. The banks of the Alt were covered in the first vicious nettle growth and, once the excitement of the day wore off, he was on fire. We were putting up at a splendid pub in Birkenhead called the Bowler Hat. Not only do they welcome dogs but the Italian manager, in direct contradiction to the general opinion of the rest of the world, actually thought Tug was wonderful and kept popping into the kitchen for titbits for the 'leetle fellow'. Like us, he had had a terrific day and slept like a log.

The following morning we met Lee, Dave, the lads and their terriers, joined this time by Dave's girlfriend Tracey, a new convert to field sports, with aquamarine fingernails, at John and Sherri Bloor's dairy farm near Holmes Chapel. John and Sherri's love of livestock is reflected in the variety of fowl they keep: Light Sussex and Old English hens and those superlative layers, Rhode Island Reds, as well as Muscovy and Aylesbury ducks, all housed in the runs behind a magnificent Elizabethan barn. It was a typical ratty place – a mixture of very old and modern farm buildings, feed stores, hen houses and duck coops. The hens and ducks are kept in several different fenced-off areas and we could see rat runs snaking between them and back to the steading. No one likes using poison. Dead rats rotting under the floor of a building or decomposing in running water are as big a health hazard to humans as live rats, and if you have a lot of dogs about the place, the risk of poisoning them makes it out of the question. The Bloors' farm was a perfect example of the service provided by the MWTLC and a good opportunity for the lads to experience life in the country for a day.

The great Duke of Beaufort once said, 'The two things I love most in life are hunting and ratting and I have never decided which I love the best.' This is a sentiment echoed by all those who have done both, and our day with the Bloors has joined the archives of treasured memories which will, I hope, sustain me in my dotage. At one stage, when we were surrounding a large chicken shed and Dave was revving his strimmer engine, we were joined by that great sportsman Gethin Jones, who organises the Cheshire County Show at Peover. 'If

The Mersey boys and guests

I was you I'd lift that shed. Let the terriers in,' says Gethin. A scaffolding pole was quickly found and thrust under the side of the shed that had been in place for perhaps forty or so years. With half a dozen of us straining on the end of the pole, it began inching upwards. The terriers were thrusting forward and Conker, so called I discovered because his face and head are always covered in bumps from the fights he has at school, was lying flat on his face in the hen shit squealing, 'I can see 'em, I can see 'em.' Clarrie, her blood thoroughly up, came charging in from point where she had been covering one of the rat runs and flung her weight on to the end of the pole. The shed shot into the air. Mercifully someone shoved a block in before it crashed down and squashed Conker and the terriers who had leapt forward into the gap. Clarrie was left rolling in the glaur, roaring with laughter.

It is a kaleidoscope of wonderful memories: Dave scrambling up a ladder to rev his strimmer into a hole halfway up an old alder tree to evict three rats that had run up inside it. Tug grabbing one under the nose of Jess as it bolted and refusing to give it up. 'Get your own bloody rat, this one's mine.' Clarrie surging up and down the shore with her hat gone and her hair blowing in the wind, lashing at rats with her shillelagh as they swam across from the island where John and Sherri have nesting boxes for mallard. The Merseyside boys, Dave and Lee lined up beside a straw stack at the end of our day to have their photographs taken, with the terriers lunging forward on their leads at the day's bag, twenty-five rats laid out in front of them. Above all I shall remember meeting six lads from Liverpool housing estates, one of which is so rough the locals refer to it as Cannibal Farm, who had perfect manners, whose terriers were beautifully looked after and handled gently and sensibly, who lacked that modern, all-encompassing expression 'attitude' and who, had I not been told their background, I would have assumed to be six well-behaved country lads. The work that Dave, Lee, Kevin and the other members of the club devote to these youngsters is incredibly admirable and an example to us all. They richly deserve the award from the Countryside Alliance, presented to Kevin at the Lowther Show by Richard Burge last year.

The MWTLC is not alone in operating rescue services and rehousing terriers that have been abandoned or whose owners cannot keep them for one reason or another. The Fell and Moorland Working Terrier Club (FMWTC), started in 1967 by a group of Cumbrian enthusiasts, offers a national rescue service for its members that extends to any breed of dog. It is the natural instinct of all dogs to hunt and most small breeds share with terriers the habit of going to ground. There is nothing quite like the anxiety of knowing that the family pet is fast below ground. The dog may have toppled into an underground stream, become jammed in an unexpectedly narrowing drainpipe, or been trapped by a cave-in. The permutations of the nightmare are endless.

Some of the FMWTC rescues have been epics requiring the deployment of diggers and dynamite, the removal of trees, even abseiling into the depths. They often involve acts of considerable bravery by volunteers who are literally prepared to move heaven and earth at any time, anywhere to save someone's pet. The considerable cost of these operations is borne by the club. Furthermore, should any dog go to ground in a badger sett, which cannot be disturbed by law, the club will negotiate for permission from the police to allow the rescue to go ahead.

These clubs are only two of the twenty-six member terrier clubs of the National Working Terrier Federation (NWTF), formed in 1984. The NWTF represents some four thousand individual members plus other affiliated organisations in England, Scotland and Wales. Together they drew up the NWTF code of conduct. This details the legal requirements that those engaged in terrier work must follow and identifies the best practices to be adhered to in order to provide a pest control service which is humane, efficient and selective and which ensures the welfare of both the working terrier and its quarry. The code is now accepted internationally and is endorsed by the major field sports and conservation organisations. The NWTF also implemented a scheme for the registration of terrier men and pest controllers. Becoming a registered terrier man is somewhat more difficult than acquiring a gun licence, but accountability is the only way to persuade the media, politicians and the public that centuries-

Showing a Border Terrier

old tried and tested practices are both essential and humane methods of controlling vermin.

During the late 1970s and 1980s, the essential use of terriers to control vermin – one that is recognised internationally – came under attack from increasingly violent protesters. Isolated terrier men, more accessible than the field on hunting days, were frequently targeted by masked hunt saboteurs. As a result, the working terrier clubs realised the importance of making the general public aware of the manner in which properly conducted terrier work is carried out, and banded together to form the NWTF.

In 1999 the NWTF produced an enormously detailed paper on the modern-day role of the working terrier in pest control which, together with other submissions from scientists, conservationists, heritage bodies and all country sports organisations, was presented to the parliamentary committee of enquiry into hunting with dogs known as the Burns Commission. Theirs was also among submissions presented to the Rural Affairs Committee of the Scottish Parliament, whose brief was to report on the Protection of Wild Mammals (Scotland) Bill. It is a sad reflection of how remote government has become from the workings of rural Britain that so much parliamentary time and taxpayers' money has been devoted to vermin control methods that are practised internationally.

Some of the NWTF member clubs are large, like the Fell and Moorland Working Terrier Club, and others, such as the Jack Russell Club of Great Britain, have links worldwide – in this case with the Jack Russell Terrier Club of America and the Jack Russell United World Federation. Some are smaller. The clubs are based in both rural and urban areas. Between them they organise hundreds of enormously popular shows. The Fell and Moorland club held 32 shows during 1999 and 111 meetings and social events. A glance through the

Winnie the Witch of Hardytown

Countryman's Weekly will show hundreds through the summer, advertising at least 45 between mid-August and the end of September as well as the increasingly popular terrier racing events. Some are terrier shows in their own right, while others are part of the attraction at much larger shows, game fairs, county fairs, point-to-points and other rural occasions.

One of the stars of these shows is Winnie the Witch of Hardytown. Winnie is a terrier bitch of the Jack Russell type. For the last four seasons Winnie has earned her keep through the winter working with the Croome and West Warwickshire Foxhounds. During the summer you will find her helping the Three Counties Mink Hounds. She has also worked with the famous David Davies Hunt in mid-Wales, an accolade afforded only to the very best. Being a working terrier hasn't spoilt her good looks. Far from being scarred or mutilated, she won the Best of Breed at Crufts in 1997 and 1999, has won five Challenge Certificates to date and is one of the highest awarded working terriers in Britain today. I have yet to meet her but from the photographs she would be an ideal bitch for Tug.

As we drove north the following day, with Tug curled up asleep in the footwell, I mentioned to Clarissa that Gethin's parting act had been to extract a promise to come down for the Cheshire Game and Angling Fair. If the foot and mouth epidemic was under control by the late summer the fair would be held on 19th August. At this stage of our journey we were driving through Cumberland, past fells bare of livestock with columns of oily black smoke rising into the sky from the pyres of burning carcasses further north. 'If the government doesn't get a grip soon,' Clarrie said prophetically, 'there won't be any shows at all.'

Throughout that long sad summer the rural economy got a taste of what life would be like if a government were successful in banning field sports. All the events that take place during the summer – the point-to-points, game fairs, terrier shows, the traditional Border Common Ridings, the gypsy horse fairs and most fishing – were cancelled, with a massive impact on the tourist economy. Eventually, with four million animals slaughtered and foot and mouth localised to certain areas, some events started to take place again and the threads of normal life were gradually picked up.

Towards the end of July Clarrie was over for the day trying out her hammer gun on some

Exploding after the lure

clays when Gethin telephoned. 'All the local farmers and landowners are solidly behind the fair going ahead. You'll see lots of old friends if you come and there'll be terrier racing. Bring that little dog of yours.' 'Terrier racing?' said Clarrie, her eyes sparkling. 'We've got three weeks. Tug must go into training. I'll get the quad. You get that fox brush I saw in your shed, and some string.'

The principle of terrier racing is to place four competing terriers in individual compartments like the start boxes for a horse race. A bicycle wheel is mounted in the middle of the boxes, with a stout cord connecting it to another wheel fifty yards away. A lure is attached to the cord and, when the doors of the compartments are lifted, the man operating the wheel at the far end winds the lure towards him. The lure disappears up a tube and the owners have all the fun of trying to catch their respective terriers. Tug can be fairly fleet of foot, as anything that invades the perimeter of his carefully marked territory will tell you, and his daily pursuit of the fox brush, tied to the quad driven by Clarissa and towed across the field behind the steading, honed both him and me to a remarkable level of fitness. Clarissa had been making careful notes of Tug's times, and as we packed to leave for Cheshire she patted me on the arm. 'We've got a winner here,' she beamed. 'There's money in that dog. Damned if I don't put my blouse on him.'

The fair is typical of the many that take place every summer throughout Britain in a normal year, offering a broad spectrum of country interests and pursuits and a wonderful opportunity for city people to understand what goes on in the countryside. There were displays of carriage driving by the Blinkers Club, a recently formed group of enthusiasts, and side-saddle riding competitions – how lovely to see a resurgence of interest in that elegant riding style. Gundog events with a big crowd watching labradors, spaniels, pointers and a whole variety of the continental hunter-pointer-retriever breeds plunging into a pond to retrieve a lure. A stall selling six shots with a catapult at china plates for 50p to raise money for Frodsham Wildfowlers' junior members. Demonstrations of muzzle-loading firearms, falconry, farriery, ferrets and fly casting. Archery and clay pigeon shooting competitions, and craft stalls selling everything for the sportsman. There were vintage vehicles, pipe bands and pole climbing, and a chainsaw demonstration. Sadly, the popular parade of hounds could not take place because of the foot and mouth.

With parts of the countryside opening up, the fair was packed and practically everyone seemed to have brought a dog. There was every variety of lurcher and terrier. Sleek and beautiful German pointers, labradors, Chesapeake Bay retrievers, lordly greyhounds and even a couple of chihuahuas, cuddled by two identically dressed young men. Tug is not a good mixer. His inability to grasp the rudiments of social graces means that he rarely leaves the farm, and he stalked through this canine multitude stiff-legged, with his head down and hackles up, muttering horribly.

'That's the sort of competitive spirit I like to see,' chuckled Clarrie as Tug snarled something unprintable at a perfectly amiable bull mastif. 'I'll buy you dinner with my winnings.'

Down at the terrier racing arena we met up with Dave Moorcroft and the Mersey boys – Conker, Snudge and the others who had been with us on our ratting expedition – as well as Lee Haslam and a whole group of lads we had never met before. Demand from the youngsters in Liverpool and the surrounding areas had created a need for another club covering all field sports, and Lee, with team leaders Paul Freeman and John McNally, had started the Northwest Fieldsports Youth Club just eight weeks previously. They already had fifteen members including an eight-year-old girl. The club's motto is 'The future', reflecting their belief that children are the future of field sports.

An enthusiastic crowd lined the sides of the arena, with a long queue of competing terriers waiting their turn. There were black Fell terriers, Patterdales, Lakelands, Borders and little yappy Norfolks. John Bloor was there with his leggy wire-haired bitch and Conker was further up the queue clinging to a smooth-haired black and white dog that looked like a half-cross Staffordshire. The noise of a hundred terriers all holding forth is terrific and the winner of each heat is usually the one who doesn't get involved in the dispute that generally takes place halfway up the course.

When Tug's turn came he was racing against Lee's Fell bitch Ferry, a chocolate Patterdale, a very showy Border and an odd-looking creature belonging to a small girl that could only have been part dachshund. I could see Clarrie in the crowd, brandishing her wallet, in earnest conversation with a swarthy little chap in a leather cap. Behind me, as I popped Tug into his start box, I could hear a group of aficionados fancying 'the little white dog with the brown ears'. Popular money was obviously on Tug. The lure was waggled in front of the boxes and there were screams of excitement from within.

Suddenly a cold hand clutched my heart. In my young day, when we had terrier racing at the local gymkhana, the lure was always a brush. This one was a stuffed canvas sock. I waved frantically at Clarrie. She waved cheerily back. The gates flew open and three terriers exploded after the lure. Tug stepped slowly into the sunlight with a look of utter disdain on his face. 'A sock?' he seemed to say. 'I'm not chasing a sock.'

CHAPTER TWO

DIVERSIFICATION IS THE NAME OF THE GAME

The last decade has been a lean one for farmers. Foreign imports, European legislation, the predominance of the supermarkets and, especially, the increased demand for cheap food have whittled away their profits. Small farmers and hill farmers like Johnny are constantly looking for new ways to increase their income. Diversification is essential for almost all of them. Whether it is the most simple kind where a farmer cuts grass for the local council or involves entirely different occupations such as part-time law or taxidermy, most are driven by a need to obtain an income from other kinds of farming or other sources altogether. Some are very successful.

My friend Johnny Noble at Ardkinglas inherited a large West Highland estate. The Glasgow shipping money that had bought and paid for it was several generations in the past. 'What, Mr Noble,' asked the bank, 'are your plans?' He replied that he would enlarge the highland herd (which pleased them) and build a sawmill (which pleased them even more). Then, he stated, 'I shall lay down an oyster bed'. When the

The mussel spats arrive with the daffodils

laughter had ceased, they smiled politely. 'Everyone is entitled, Mr Noble, to a hobby.'

Now Johnny Noble knew there had been oysters on the loch in the past. During the war his job as a young lad was to gather oyster shells from the shore and grind them into grit for the chickens. 'Every oyster shell,' cried his father, 'is a bullet for Hitler!' The stories of how Johnny and his business partner Andrew Lane laid the oyster beds are legend, and they were enthusiastically supported by a Highlands and Islands Enterprise Board who knew even less than they did. What I remember was attending a Food Fair at Olympia in 1982 to be confronted by Johnny saying, 'Taste this.' This was one of the best oysters I have ever eaten.

Johnny and I went to Loch Fyne to see the oyster beds. The oysters are acquired as spat from Lord Creran near Oban and reared on the shore of the loch on large racks. Loch Fyne is a tidal sea loch, so the tide comes in and covers the molluscs and then goes out again, leaving them exposed to the weather. Interestingly, on a hot day they can endure very high

Oyster beds at Loch Fyne

'. . . mussels alive, alive oh'

temperatures with impunity, and where the sunlight touches the shells, this can be seen in shell development as ridging and changes in colour. We sampled oysters straight from the loch, plump and tasting slightly of salt, then went to the filtering and cleaning tanks where the oysters are kept in pumped loch water under ultraviolet light (mainly to reassure the public, because the water contains few impurities).

I also went out to the new mussel beds. All they do is put down ropes, 'before,' as Andrew Lane said, 'the daffodils come out', and the wild mussel spat, which are skimming around the loch looking for somewhere to perch, go, 'Whoopee! New houses!' and cling to the ropes, where they grow and mature very quickly. Because they are wild, Loch Fyne mussels are a nice orange colour rather than the pasty white you find in some farmed mussels.

Today the name of Loch Fyne Oysters is famous around the world. The Sea Food Fair is an annual must, and any traveller up the west coast of Scotland who fails to stop at the restaurant at Cairndow is severely lacking in love of food. They have recently become involved in a series of restaurants around the country, for which they source all the fish and seafood. These restaurants are not in fashionable London but often in traditional oyster-eating areas such as Loughton in Essex. As the Romans proved long ago, oysters travel extremely well. British oysters were much prized and exported to Rome in barrels of seawater. The Emperor Nero boasted that he could eat any oyster and say from which part of his empire it had come. French supermarkets are full of Loch Fyne smoked salmon. I have seen their kippers in rural Devon and it was for their exports to Hong Kong and many other countries that they won the Queen's Award for Exports. What was once a smallish West Highland estate is now an empire employing not only Johnny's family but also most of the people in the area – a happy story of diversification!

Cheesemaking is an important activity for some dairy farmers but our governments do nothing to support the artisan cheese industry. In 1995 a government department nearly closed down Humphrey Errington, a successful small Scottish cheesemaker who makes Lanarkshire Blue and other cheeses from both cows' and ewes' milk, for alleged breaches of various regulations. Mr Errington did not slink away quietly but stood with his back to the wall and fought them through the courts. We all fundraised like mad and signed petitions all over Scotland. The courts upheld Mr Errington's case and the authority was vanquished but learnt no lessons. Humphrey Errington continues in his cheese production, still using unpasteurised milk and with his spirits undaunted. Fortunately the publicity did not harm him and the quality of his cheese remains unchanged, but the government didn't amend the regulations.

The Curtesses at Bonchester Bridge were a great success story. They originally bought a Jersey cow to provide cream for their soft fruit, but they started making cheese when the fruit failed one wet summer and they were left with a lot of cream. The result was the highly prized award-winning Bonchester cheese. This was diversification at its best, and part of an artisan cheese revival which swept the country when the bottom fell out of the milk market and farmers needed to find alternative uses for their milk. However, repeated legislation on the use of unpasteurised milk in cheese, largely led by concern about listeria, drove the Curtesses to such distraction that they halted production. If you look in a supermarket now, you will find only a few unpasteurised French cheeses and no unpasteurised British ones. The reason given is the avoidance of listeria, which is somewhat ironic considering that, as I was told a while ago, 90 per cent of listeria outbreaks in the UK came from cold ready-made meals or sandwiches supplied by the various supermarket chains.

The grocer and cheesemonger Ian Mellis, who has a fantastic cheese shop in Edinburgh's Victoria Street, sells cheese from all over the UK. He tells me that unpasteurised British cheese production has fallen drastically and he finds that increasingly his suppliers come from Ireland, whose government supports the industry along with all farmed food production. Ian Mellis himself is a unique success story. He has cheese shops in Edinburgh and in Glasgow, a coffee roaster's, and two old-fashioned grocer's shops selling teas, coffees, butter, eggs and bacon, some other meat and organic fruit and vegetables. Thus did the first Sainsbury's start, but these are different times. He is one of the few local grocers to buck the supermarket trend.

Farm shops are an increasingly common form of diversification. Many of the soft fruit and vegetable farmers who grow for the shops and supermarkets have also developed a sideline in selling direct to the consumer. From the consumer's point of view, the nearer from picking or digging to eating, the better the taste. We went to visit a splendid woman called Caroline Dickinson who has a thriving farm shop just outside Newcastle. She sells vegetables and soft fruit from her own farm and runs a tea room that uses her produce to make cooked foods. It is well worth buying from farm shops like hers that sell their own produce or that of neighbouring farms: they are an ideal source of locally produced food that is in season. We can now buy virtually everything except broad beans and cherries all year round, and most of it tastes of nothing. I have returned to eating food by season and it has revitalised my interest.

Historically food had to follow the seasons. The fasts of Lent, for example, protected the breeding stock, encouraged the eating of the antiscorbutics that prevent scurvy, and fitted in with the first fish runs. Thomas Tusser, writing in 1557, gives the verse on seasonal food on the page opposite.

Supplemented with worts and greens culled from the hedgerow or the garden plot, this is the basis of a balanced diet. I can't stand tasteless modern lettuce but a salad with hawthorn leaves, ground elder and Good King Henry, all weeds really, is very good indeed and actually does you some good.

THOMAS TUSSER, FIVE HUNDREDE POINTES OF GOOD HUSBANDRIE (1557)

A Plot set downe, for farmers quiet,
as time requires, to frame his diet;
With sometime fish, and sometime fast,
that household store, may longer last.

Lent
Let Lent well kept, offend not thee,
for March and Aprill breeders be,
Spend herring first, saue saltfish last:
for saltfish is good, when Lent is past.

Easter
When Easter comes, who knowes not than,
that Veale and Bakon, is the man.
And Martilmas beefe, doth beare good tack:
when countrie folk, doe dainties lack.

Midsomer
When Mackrell ceaseth from the seas,
John Baptist brings, grasse beefe and pease.

Mihelmas
Fresh herring plentie, Mihell brings,
with fatted Crones [mutton] and such old things.

Hallomas
All Saintes doe laie, for porke and souse [pickled pork]:
for sprats and spurlings [smelts], for their house.

Christmas
At Christmas play, and make good cheere:
for Christmas comes but once a yeere.

* * *

The land doth will, the Sea doth wish,
spare sometime flesh, and feede of fish:

Where fish is scant, and fruite of trees:
Supplie that want, with butter and cheese.

Through most of history the diet of the labouring man was made up of 'white meats', as dairy protein products such as cheese or curds were known, supplemented with bacon from the cottage pig. Until the legislation about keeping a pig near a dwelling house changed in 1910, a great many pigs were still raised. My father kept pigs during the war but my siblings wouldn't eat the first lot for reasons of sentiment. He called the next two Goering and Rommel and they were eaten with alacrity. The swine feasts were a huge adventure and as a senior surgeon he did the butchery himself. Three years ago I acquired two Tamworths but was not allowed to slaughter them even though they were for my own consumption, and when they came back from the abattoir they were minus a lot of the interesting bits from which I could have made black pudding or andouilles (sausages made from chitterlings).

A pig is the perfect beast to raise for a family as everything is edible except the squeal. It provides the makings of a huge variety of different dishes, from joints and chops to sausages and bacon, ham and pork (salted, pickled or fresh) and of course lard for the cooking. The cottage pig, fed on scraps and put to the boar in season, would provide a family with both food and an income, and was turned out into the woods in the autumn to feast on the beech and oak mast, thus keeping the woodlands clear. The Worshipful Company of Butchers, of which I am proud to be a liveryman, parades a boar's head to the Mansion House every autumn to present to the Lord Mayor as a token that the autumn pig-killing and salting has begun.

Peter Gott was a cheesemaker until his brother gave him some pigs for his twenty-seventh birthday. Now he farms 160 wild boar and other pigs on 27 acres of woodland on the Cumbrian coast. He is a happy farmer who always wears breeches, red stockings and a brown Derby (a type of bowler) at shows. He sells fat bacon, wild boar pancetta, even a Dunmow flitch. This is a rolled cut of bacon with a deep layer of fat which in Dunmow in Essex is still awarded to the couple in the parish who have fought least during the year. His bacon is wonderful. I buy pounds of it at a time and put it in my fridge: it keeps for ever, almost literally. I once kept some for a year as an experiment and it was perfect. This is not as surprising as it seems, since bacon was originally designed to be stored through the winter in a cool larder.

Everything is edible bar the oink

Johnny and I went to see Peter at his farm. The majority of his wild boars are of German or Polish stock, but a few years ago he bought some Russian boars out of curiosity. They are easily distinguishable by their longer snouts, red aggressive eyes, sandy colouring and slighter build. Wild boar are surprisingly small, given the stories of ravening beasts charging from the forest breathing mutilation and death. Skipping happily round the wood stacks at the edge of the woodland which is their Cumbrian home, they seem friendly creatures. Then the head sow will turn on some younger pig, or one is taken to see Boris, the main Russian boar, thrashing his huge tusks against the bars of his stall, and it becomes obvious that this is a dangerous wild beast indeed. When the Victorian game laws came into force, there were no wild boar left in Britain, and so they were not catered for in the legislation. Consequently, any wild boar sold in Britain has to be taken to the abattoir to be slaughtered. No fun for Peter, especially when his beasts are larger than normal at the moment because of the foot and mouth restrictions. They have to be put in crushes to be transported on the lorries, and the staff at the abattoir are not

Peter Gott with his wild boar

keen on handling them. Peter is into added value. When asked why his products are expensive he points out that they take three years from birth to plate, and with the Parma-type hams one loses a third of the product in shrinkage and wastage. Peter sells all types of pork products, and he still sells Cumbrian cheese. He eats all his own stuff, is as fit as a flea and much lusted after by the ladies.

Making wild boar pancetta.

It is a little known fact that Johnny is a splendid cook. His father (the Walter to whom we dedicated the last book) was, despite his size and robust approach to life, the most sensitive and subtle of cooks – a skill his son has inherited. Every so often Johnny makes a sally into the realm of preserves. I for one will never forget the year he decided to turn the remaining unsold geese from his son's Christmas labours into *confit d'oie*. A great aura of excitement hovered over the whole project, with much toing and froing of recipes. Johnny is a rigorous perfectionist, so there were lengthy heated discussions over cooking temperatures and methods of dividing the carcasses. When Johnny is energised about something, his marmalade curls sparkle with a life of their own. By the end of this project they were so crackling with electricity that they could easily have generated the power needed to cook the geese.

His wife Mary had retired to bed with a nasty bout of flu, so Johnny had complete dominion in the kitchen. I was not invited to help, though I did receive various expletive phone calls during the session. It was a beginning-to-end adventure: he killed the geese, plucked them, dressed them, cut them up and cooked them himself, and the end result was a great many large Kilner jars of *confit d'oie*, rich with goose fat and perfectly cooked. Men are not known for their abilities in the domestic department, so it cast something of a blight over the event when Mary tottered weakly down to fill a hot-water bottle and measured her length on the one smear of goose fat that had escaped Johnny's Herculean attempts to clean up. Still, we all had a happy time making cassoulet for some time to come. A farmers' market would have been a perfect venue to sell the fruits of his labours, producing a nice profit and limiting the flatulence among his friends. One can really only eat so many haricot beans.

In the days when we were self-supporting, the wealth from the nation's food production was engendered in its markets. Every great town had a weekly or even twice-weekly market to which the country people brought their produce. Markets were a central part of the medieval way of life and regulations abounded for controlling traffic or waggons going home empty. Forestalling, the act of buying food on its way to market to sell at a higher price, was severely punished and in the East End markets the cleaning up was done by the Tantony pig. These creatures, wearing a bell and the badge of St Anthony's Hospital, roamed free around the markets and were thus fed on the parish for the benefit of the hospital.

Over and above this were the huge fairs like the Nottingham Goose Fair to which thousands of Michaelmas geese were walked. Their feet were dipped in tar to protect them. What an amazing sight it must have been: great white flocks being moved along the roads at a snail's pace, honking and babbling. Similarly turkeys were walked to London until well into the last century to be sold at Smithfield for the Christmas trade. There are drovers' roads around the country as old as time. A friend tells me that during the Second World War, when there was no petrol, the farmers in the Scottish Borders drove the cattle to the market towns over distances of ten miles or more on the drovers' roads and organised the auctions themselves. So it is not so very long since local produce was sold in local markets rather than being distributed from a central point miles from the purchaser.

I took a break from writing this morning and went out to the Edinburgh farmers' market which now occupies Castle Terrace twice-monthly. It is held on a windswept site in a cold car park because the residents of the Grassmarket objected to its being sited in its obvious home. (I should tell you that the Grassmarket, where I have my shop, is not Belgravia or Morningside: I spend much time chasing the drunks off my own doorstep, but there we are.) Despite its location and the cold, damp day, the market was well attended by producers and customers alike. I bought wonderful clotted cream from Jean Stichell, venison kidneys and sausages from a farm just outside Perth, and a boiling chicken (almost unobtainable elsewhere) from a farmer's wife from Yarrow who started raising chickens when the price of livestock dropped. She adds value by making curried chicken sausages and rissoles with lemon and thyme, among many other dishes. There were eggs, butter, mutton – some free range, some organic, but all locally produced. There were also delicious strawberries that the supermarkets wouldn't take because they are not all the same shape and size, locally smoked

Geese were walked for miles to Michaelmas goosefairs

trout and so much more. I talked to customers and suppliers alike. The customers were delighted to see the market back after the winter and the foot and mouth outbreak, and wondered how they had ever done without it, and the suppliers were full of the enthusiasm that no government or other authority can destroy. As one producer said, one of the best bits was that she could talk to her customers and find out what they wanted.

I have spent most of my life bemoaning the loss of produce markets in this country and grinding my teeth when people returned from the Continent singing the praises of markets in France, Spain or Italy. It was when visiting America on a publicity tour some five years ago that hope sprang to life. In the 1980s America saw a huge food resurgence known as 'new wave' cooking. This began in California and was attributable to five chefs: Alice Waters, Jeremiah Tower, Wolfgang Puck, Deborah Maddison and Mark Miller. They took the established rules of various cuisines, smashed them, then mixed and matched them.

Over the centuries, every nation's cookery has developed particular sets of traditions which define them, such as serving lamb with mint sauce, or duck with green peas, or the fact that in Italy no chicken is served with pasta. One exception to this last rule is found in Trieste, home of the Austro-Hungarian navy – Italy was of course part of that empire – on the Yugoslavian border, where the central European habit of serving chicken with noodles was translated into a form of Bolognese sauce made with chicken and served with spaghetti. This is an early example of what the new wavers were trying to achieve by overruling all the old traditions. At worst their food was a horrid mishmash, but when they got it right it was the most exciting food revolution for two hundred years and it began in the United States, home of the giant supermarket.

Alice Waters at Chez Panisse was heavily influenced by the writings of Elizabeth David, with her emphasis on using fresh ingredients produced within the locality, and in order to obtain the quality of ingredients she required, she persuaded local farmers to grow for her alone. As there was a substantial surplus to her requirements, the farmers set up local markets which became a feature of Californian life. While in Los Angeles I was taken to two of them by friends and it was a heady experience. In the course of my endless television interviews I was often asked what I liked best about America and invariably I waxed eloquent about these markets.

I returned to England disheartened, but I am fortunate to have a great friend in Henrietta Green. Henrietta and I grew up in the same part of London and played in the same playground, of which the small cemetery was the main attraction, but we didn't become friends until much later. Perhaps in our mutual love of food we were both influenced by the fact that St John's Wood, where we lived, had a high street with very good food shops. There were several butchers and two fishmongers, as well as some greengrocers run by a colourful Sicilian family called Salamone. As befits a largely Jewish area, there was also a brilliant delicatessen.

For many years, Henrietta was the lone voice in the wilderness crying the cause of the small producer when the supermarkets stalked the land unchallenged. Her professional reference book *British Food Finds* (1986) pointed the way and won many awards. Then she moved into the public forum with *Food Routes* (1988), published with the RAC, and finally *Food Lovers' Guide to Britain* (1993). For all these books, Henrietta toured the country searching out the best local food suppliers. I once went out on the road with her for a day, thinking it would be a nice outing, but so energetic and rigorous was she in her cross-examination of the suppliers we visited that I was quite exhausted. Lastly to date came her Food Lovers' Fairs (the first in St Christopher's Place in 1995) when she took her finest suppliers out to meet the people. I was part of her army and marched loyally with her, selling books and later being an attraction myself. The fairs are usually held in beautiful settings and I have taken to camping with the other stall holders so as not to miss the fun. We have great barbecues: Peter Gott once barbecued a whole wild boar (the beast had escaped and he had to shoot it, which made it unsaleable by law as it hadn't gone through an abattoir).

Henrietta and I talked about farmers' markets and worked to that end (she more rigorously and effectively than I). The first English farmers' market was started in Bath in 1997 by Rob Weston, who had also gone to America and admired what he saw. Bath council proved more amenable than most and so it all began. In 1999 Henrietta invited me to be patron of the Farmers' Markets Association, an honour I accepted with pride.

The farmers' markets have grown and grown. The first in Scotland was in Perth in April 1999 and is now a strong monthly market and a way of life. John Scott, the founder of the Ayr market (in the car park of a supermarket), found himself elected to the Scottish Parliament. At a market I attended in Sutton Coldfield in Birmingham I came across a man who had a stand of seventy walnut trees and couldn't sell his product because the major users bought from France alone! The produce at farmers' markets comes from local producers who are usually based within a thirty-mile radius of the market, and the food hygiene laws are rigorously enforced. I have visited these markets up and down the country and bought wonderful local sausages, cheeses, jams, tracklements and preserves, as well as breads, all sorts of meat and poultry and, of course, fruit and vegetables.

Organic food is the great new development. The supermarkets have latched on to it as they once did to the word healthy. The EU regulation on organic production states that you must not describe organic food as healthy and, given the depths to which the latter word has sunk, that's probably a good idea. However, I don't think that is what the EU had in mind! Lady Eve Balfour, who had a spiritual awakening over an East Lothian compost heap, was an early organic farmer and one of the founders of the Soil Association. She predicted that poorly raised food would be reflected in the deteriorating health of the nation's children. The Prince

A chance for the farmer to meet the urban customer

of Wales is a great champion of organic farming in modern times. Jennifer Paterson and I went to Highgrove to film 'Two Fat Ladies' and I was completely overwhelmed by the quality of the produce and the quiet efficiency with which all the bits fitted seamlessly together: the osiers grown to filter the water were harvested and woven into baskets; the clover grown for winter feed fed nutrients back into the soil. I could go on ad infinitum.

This is organic farming at its best, but beware, because while the Soil Association rigorously monitors British organic produce it can be a different tale overseas. Third World organic produce is not always trustworthy. I have heard that registration can take as little as three days; this means that plants may have been sown as modified, doused with weedkiller and harvested as organic. This is, of course, the worst case scenario but believe me, it happens. European organics are not as closely controlled as our own. While France and Germany measure up, I understand that some poorer countries have a mere three-month registration period. However, by and large, the organic movement can only be a benefit, decreasing as it does the use of chemicals in food production. Buy organic, therefore, but be careful to check the country of origin.

The Highgrove beef that Jennifer and I cooked was superlative in both flavour and quality, and what you need to look for is meat that has been properly butchered and hung. My friend Jan McCourt at Northfield Farm in Rutland produces wonderful Dexter cattle, Berkshire and British saddleback pigs, and fine lambs. He is instrumental in disseminating information about the special exemptions that are particularly relevant to rare and old breeds of cattle, albeit under rigorous qualifying conditions: in certain circumstances cattle can be slaughtered later than the more usual thirty months brought in as part of the BSE precautions. Older breeds mature more slowly and so take longer to raise, but farmers are not always told about the special provisions, despite their importance under the foot and mouth restrictions. There is no doubt in my mind that the old breeds invariably taste better than modern ones, particularly when they are grass-fed. The animals that come through Buccleuch Beef, the co-operative formed by the Duke of Buccleuch for his beef tenants to sell direct to restaurants and selected butchers, are all grass-fed and many of them are from the hills. This scheme proved so successful that they had to include selected non-Buccleuch tenants to supply the orders, all in Scotland, and they took the decision to build a new abattoir at Castle Douglas, one of the areas which took the brunt of the foot and mouth. Both Jan McCourt and Peter Gott, along with many other good producers, sell at Borough Market by London Bridge every Friday and Saturday, and the Rare Breeds Survival Trust has a list of accredited butchers on its website (www.rare-breed.com).

Small farmers produce food that is a joy to eat and cook. Heal Farm was producing rare breed meat as early as the 1980s and delivering by post around the country. Pipers Farm began as one farming family selling their produce to the public and now incorporates a whole Devon valley into the co-operative equation. I remember so well the first Pipers Farm product I bought, at Henrietta's Christmas Fair in St Christopher's Place in 1995. I had virtually given up eating chicken because it tasted horrible and had no texture but I bought a chicken breast stuffed with apricots because a friend had asked me to bring something back for dinner and there wasn't much else left. The instructions said it should be cooked for one hour. I remarked that it would be cooked to extinction, but Ann Piper looked at me sternly. 'Think back,' she cried, and then I remembered that there had come a time when, although I was cooking chicken for the same length of time, I was finding them overcooked. What had changed was not me nor my oven but the chickens.

For battery chickens, the average time from egg to table is only six weeks (and may sometimes be as little as five weeks). By contrast, organic chickens reared for meat cannot be slaughtered until they are at least ten weeks old or, for some breeds, at least eleven and a half weeks (eighty-one days). I also remembered the fine Cumbrian smoker Richard Woodall saying that he couldn't smoke chickens properly any more as the new types had flesh that didn't adhere to the bone tightly and mortification set in too easily. I took this chicken breast home and cooked it as advised and was reminded how good chicken can be. After eating one of Linda Dick's slowly reared free-range chickens at my house, our researcher Lindsay Gilmour made the very important point that we have only a generation to play with before people are so convinced that chicken tastes like polystyrene that they won't eat the real thing.

Much of the chicken we eat is imported from Third World countries where it may be raised in conditions that are unsatisfactory (to put it politely). Personally, I wouldn't knowingly eat a Third World chicken because the producers' attention to hygiene, feeding habits and animal welfare is not on a level with ours. We import something like 42 per cent of our meat, and 80 per cent of that is poultry. Pork is the meat of which we consume most (chicken is the second most popular meat). Curiously, only 14 per cent of pork is sold through supermarkets, I have been told, as opposed to 38 per cent of other meat. Allowing imports of cheap food is, safety apart, a real strain on our farmers. Domestic produce is subject to legislation imposed – usually quite rightly – to increase food safety and improve animal welfare, and the costs of meeting the regulations has to be borne for the most part by the farmers. To allow our farmers to be undercut by cheap imports is unfair and a scandal.

The last few years have been grim for farmers. In many cases the farmers' markets and farm shops have allowed them to hang on and survive. They have also shown people what food should taste like and provided a valuable link betwen town and country which may help heal the rift that has opened up in recent decades.

CHAPTER THREE

A Dog, a Woman and a Chestnut Tree

There is probably no more satisfying occupation on a late October day than planting trees. Autumn always has a buzz of primitive excitement about it. Somehow you can feel nature tugging the last of summer's goodness and energy out of the land, drawing its defences round itself and preparing for winter's challenges. I never find autumn melancholy. There is a brooding defiance in the glorious colours of this time of the year: the last inky blackberries, scarlet rowans, the deeper reds of rosehip and hawthorn, and above all the golds, bronze, russets and ochre of the fallen leaves.

Soon it will be Hallowe'en – the old pagan ceremony of Samhuinn, a thanksgiving for the harvest and a plea to the gods for protection through the winter. It was the start of the Celtic new year and a festival of the dead. Samhuinn was quite the biggest bash in the Celtic calendar. It featured an orgy of sacrifice to Cernunnos, the antler-headed god of the underworld, and unless one had fallen foul of the Druids, everyone had a spectacular time. I love the stark eeriness of it all.

An ancient musty smell rose from the ground as I dug in the spade, excavating a hole twelve inches deep and a spade's width square.

Having carefully spread the ash sapling's roots, I began tramping back the loose earth round them. Just before replacing the square of turf, I pressed a handful of sheep's daggings (the balls of dirty wool round a ewe's back end) into the soil. This will provide some protection against frost and a little fertilisation. I placed the plastic tube that keeps the rabbits at bay over the sapling, and tapped in the supporting stake just as a mist started to creep up from the river, filling the spiders' webs on a nearby gorse bush with drops of silver moisture. I had planted thirty broad-leaved saplings – hazel, ash and oak – in a cluster at the top of a steep bank, courtesy of the Countryside Premium Scheme. Eventually little birds will nest here, I thought to myself. Wood warblers or pretty redstarts. The odd pheasant might provide a sporting shot for a gun down below, and the little copse is well placed for a fox to lie up in during the day, once a bit of cover grows. Glowing with the sense of a job well done, I walked back through the gloaming towards the house.

There are some lovely old trees on the land below the hill that runs down to the river: towering Caledonian pines and beeches; larches all tortured and bent by the wind; ashes,

Setting off to plant a rowan

alders and oak. Some of the oak trees are incredibly ancient, with massive trunks and monstrous limbs groping down to the ground. With a little imagination it is easy to envisage this valley when it was part of the great forest of Jed and much of Britain was wooded.

When the Normans appeared, an aerial view of Britain would have shown an island almost completely covered in forest, with some big marshy areas in the east. The fertile valleys were surrounded by thousands of acres of scrubby, stunted trees giving way to barren moorland in the north. Villages were small and isolated, the houses often clustered conveniently close to rivers (water was the least onerous form of transport), and connected to the few larger towns by the remains of Roman roads and winding Saxon tracks. Around the towns with their castles were large patches of forest clearance, and scattered across England, particularly south of the Wash, were sixty thousand acres of heathland created by prehistoric and Anglo-Saxon farmers. One of the last remaining areas where primitive iron smelters made their clumsy tools and ragged husbandmen cleared the scrub for their pigs and tiny flocks of milking sheep was the Ashdown Forest (many areas of heathland were termed forests simply because that was the word used to denote a royal hunting preserve).

Deer, wild boar, wolves and felons bred in the forests and no one travelled through them alone, but they provided everything the early communities needed. Every part of the tree had its use, and the wildlife was hunted for food and skins, but there was no attempt at woodland or wildlife management. In Anglo-Saxon times, hunting was a slaphappy affair. Woodland animals were driven towards a funnel-shaped dead end: a bog, perhaps, or a narrow valley, or a trap made from wattle fencing. William the Conqueror, with his insatiable love of hunting, introduced scientific hunting methods perfected in Normandy. Hunting 'par force', a highly skilled technique, used relays of scenting hounds until a particular beast, a deer or boar previously selected for culling by the huntsman, was turned at bay and dispatched. This form of hunting, involving the control of the game population in the royal forests, can be said to be the earliest form of woodland management.

By the Middle Ages there were 143 royal forests, covering over half a million acres. Stretching from Somerset to the Dornoch Firth, the forestal rights belonged to the kings of England and Scotland, but many of them were franchised to nobles or the Church, whose responsibility it was to ensure that their stocks of game were in the best possible physical health. The Crown expected a certain number of venison carcasses annually and the franchisees never knew when the king and his retinue might turn up expecting first-rate sport.

The management of woodland (or indeed moorland) deer has changed very little through the centuries. Overstocking of animals leads to overgrazing, with consequent damage to grass and trees. This in turn leads to loss of condition, size and carcass quality in the animals due to scarcity of food. A balanced ratio of animals to available natural growth over a given area relieves grazing pressure and potential animal suffering, but this can only be achieved by selective culling. The same practices applied in the private forests belonging to nobles. Then as now, the management of wildlife was in every landlord's best interest.

Wood continued to be an enormously valuable commodity throughout the medieval period. The countryside still appeared to be a sea of wildwood and forest, teeming with game and containing a multitude of isolated communities, but trees were being felled at an alarming rate. As the population expanded, demands on the forest escalated. More and more timber (particularly oak) was required for building houses and, during the reigns of Henry VIII and Elizabeth I, for ships, and firewood was needed on a commercial scale for smelting. Felling was concentrated in areas within easy access of transport and close to centres of population, or where smelting was an important activity. As the trees were cleared, the land was used for grazing and for sheep walks. Sheep farming was a major industry. Indeed the country's economy was based on wool.

Individual villages and farms preserved woodland for their own many needs, but there was little or no attempt at replanting after felling. Where trees were being felled on a large scale, deer and other game were protected in the palisaded parks attached to any medieval manor of substance. Woodland played an important role in manorial land management. It provided cover for a diversity of game and was therefore a source of food, as well as supplying fuel for heating and the materials for estate maintenance. By the fifteenth century, so much forestry had been cut down in the vicinity of towns that an urgent, but largely unfulfilled, need to replant was recognised. It was in these parks that the only really effective rotational replanting was conducted.

Cromwell's soldiers devastated the deer parks, smashing down the palisade fences and pillaging the woodland. Those deer that were not slaughtered escaped into the wild, living on the heaths and forests. These depredations continued during the Commonwealth. After the Restoration, large areas of hardwood were cut down by private landlords to pay for debts incurred during the Civil War, but the main reason for the destruction of wildwood and forest that accelerated in the late seventeenth century was the pressing need for domestic and, increasingly, industrial fuel. John Evelyn, the Restoration diarist, vehemently denounced the 'exhorbitance and increase of devouring iron mills', particularly in Kent, Surrey and Sussex. Unless something were done about it, he wrote glumly, 'our woods will be exhausted and England ruined'.

It was a prophetic statement. The Agricultural and Industrial Revolutions of the eighteenth and nineteenth centuries altered the landscape out of all recognition. Tons of fuel were needed as trade opened up and industry expanded, but at the beginning of the century coal mining had scarcely begun. Mined coal and sea coal (coal washed up on the shore from an underwater seam) was extremely difficult to transport except by boat. At this time our road system was deplorable. Most roads were impassable during the winter or heavy summer rain, so any town that was not near a navigable river relied entirely on home-grown fuel. As more woodland was cleared, improved farming practices swallowed up the land, and mixed farming with livestock and crop rotation created a need for fencing. Mile upon mile of hedging was planted, and about two million acres of common grazing, heath and woodland were enclosed between 1696 and 1795.

As heathland was enclosed and woodland felled, the red deer released from their manorial parks by Cromwell's troops migrated north and west, searching for sheltered habitat. The majority lingered for a short while with their Border cousins in the remains of the last great

Red deer

forests of Jed and Ettrick, their delicate ears twitching at the thud of woodmen's axes and the crash of falling timber. Moving north again, as these too were felled, woodland deer adapted to live on the open highlands, herding together for security. This behavioural pattern is unique among European red deer. Others found habitats on Dartmoor and Exmoor.

Returning monarchists brought back an innovation in shooting that was eventually to change the landscape again. On the Continent, sportsmen shot birds on the wing as well as on the ground. Shooting flying, as it was called, was initially pretty ineffective in Britain due to the inadequacies of guns at the time, but became popular as their design improved. Partridges had previously been the most accessible game but now hedgerows provided cover for pheasants, drawing them out of the woods to feed. With the development of the springer spaniel and lighter gun barrels, pheasants became a sporting target. During the early eighteenth century, copses began to be planted at the end of each hedge line, attracting pheasants from the larger woods by providing them with a convenient night roost.

Meanwhile, hardwoods were planted by the newly rich. After the Industrial Revolution, woodland ceased to be wild and natural. All but a few isolated pockets of wildwood had been felled, and the new plantings were manicured and manmade. This was the great age of the entrepreneur: merchants, ironmasters, brickmakers and lawyers made fortunes in Britain and the dominions. They bought country estates, laid out parks and settled down to a social life in the country which revolved around field sports, particularly foxhunting. Woodland was planted for its aesthetic value and, looking to the future, carefully managed for a commercial return. In the short term, it provided cover for game. The Georgians had a wonderful eye for enhancing the landscape, emphasising the curvature of a hill or a distant skyline by selective woodland planting, and many spectacular works by Capability Brown and Humphry Repton, the great eighteenth-century landscape gardeners, exist to this day.

As the road system improved and the landscape opened up, horse breeding and equestrian skills were constantly evolving. The hunter was bred to meet the need for a faster, more versatile horse and, together with the new hard-driving breed of foxhound, enabled the horseman to take part in cross-country riding over a completely unpredictable route dictated by the fox. Hunting country now covered a much bigger area than before with a wider section of the community being involved. Landowner, farmer and tenant hunted together and all were enthusiastically involved in supporting local hunts by planting and preserving cover for foxes.

There was a belated flurry of frantic hardwood replanting early in the nineteenth century, after the demand for wood to build Nelson's navy had highlighted the lack of mature trees to maintain our sea power. Admiral St Vincent, obsessed with the idea of the navy failing to defend our shores through a lack of timber, went everywhere with a bag of acorns, planting one wherever he saw a spare patch of ground.

Part of the garden created by Capability Brown at Stowe

Victorian moneybags continued parkland planting with their gloomy exotics, dark pines and rhododendrons. More woodland planting, this time as pheasant cover on a large scale, came with improvements in shotgun design. As late as the middle of the nineteenth century, time-consuming muzzle loading was replaced by an invention which enabled a gun to be loaded at the breech – the barrels pivoted open just in front of the trigger guard, enabling cartridges to be inserted – and thus reloaded quickly. This meant that high-flying, driven birds could now be shot. Circular woods were planted for battue driving, followed by a massive quantity of pine trees, chosen because they made quick growth, with shrubs, rhododendrons and laurels planted as wind breaks on elevated ground to give pheasants height when they were driven towards guns. Specific planting of game cover, designed to produce sporting birds,

A covey of grouse

escalated in the early part of the twentieth century as the practice of shooting driven birds became increasingly popular, but now hardwoods were mixed in among the pines.

Shooting driven grouse evolved because of the breech loader, but grouse moors as we know them today have a longer history. Graziers coming north in search of more sheep walks in the early eighteenth century had used burning, the oldest form of plant regeneration, on the heaths and moorlands of northern England and Scotland. By repeatedly burning on a rotational basis, the even mat of different growths of heather so familiar to tourists today was created. This provided palatable grazing not only for the hefted hill flocks but also for grouse.

Visiting sportsmen had been coming up to Scotland since about 1800 to walk up grouse and blackcock and to fish for salmon. Sporting tenants renting areas of moor noticed that grazing tenants, with their rotational burning policy, had far larger stocks of grouse. They began to adopt the same methods and discovered that sheep and grouse complement each other. Sheep open up paths along which young grouse can move before they are flying properly. They break light snow cover and frost so the grouse can feed (in hard weather you will always see grouse following sheep). They also assist in controlling heather growth by grazing and in re-seeding by dislodging seeds in their passage through the heather. Today, with hill farming incomes at an all-time low, it is the keepering community and shooting fraternity who bear the major costs of heather moorland management.

A yellow labrador retrieving

I have been lucky always to have farmed where there has been a broad horizon, with the stock practically wild, and nature has felt at home. Most of it has been on the moors of southern Scotland but there was a period when I farmed hardy Romney ewes on the north Kent marshes and had a profusion of wildfowl to keep me company. I grew up in Sussex with the beautiful endless curve of the South Downs as my view and, since there were family farms in Northumberland, the wild, lovely Cheviot Hills were added to my perspective. I have also been fortunate to know well an area of land that has changed little since William the Conqueror first saw it shortly after 1066.

The Ashdown Forest, in the high weald of Sussex, is less than fifty miles from the centre of London and is one of the last remaining ancient heaths. My mother's family came from here and as a child I spent many happy holidays on this enchanted fragment of pre-Norman old England. Among the gorse, bracken and heather, birches, scrub oaks, beech and holly, there are badgers, foxes and deer living just as they did then. Hedgehogs, moles and shrews. Voles and rare mice. Bats and many little song birds rarely seen elsewhere. The huge range of insects, plant life and mammals exists as a national treasure to remind us of what was once commonplace. That this tract of ancient land should survive unspoilt in one of the most densely populated areas of the country is a miracle of the complexities of Norman forest law and the stubborn Sussex character.

The history of the forest is one glorious row that rumbled non-stop between 1275 and the end of the nineteenth century. The local lords of the manor and the master of the forest, the king's representative, were in constant litigation with the commoners. In brief, under the feudal system, the king apportioned rights of grazing over certain heaths to his nobles and the Church. The serfs, who did all the work, had similar rights. These were in perpetuity and went with land tenure. The commoners' rights included the strictly controlled right to graze stock and the right of pannage (grazing for pigs), as well as the rights to collect fallen branches and furze for firewood, and to cut bracken for bedding – a valuable commodity in those days – and heather and turves for roofing.

Ashdown Forest

Although the depredations of successive monarchs reduced the forest from an area which stretched from Crawley to Pevensey, the commoners have never given up without a struggle. It nearly went altogether during the reign of Charles II, when he made a concerted but unsuccessful attempt to put the forest under plough, but it was the contentious issue of the commoners' right to cut bracken, something that appears frequently in the mounds of litigation over the centuries connected with Forest rights, that actually saved the Ashdown Forest. In 1876, the then lord of the manor, who owned the land, took several tenant farmers to court for cutting bracken. It was as a result of this case that a Board of Conservators (of which my grandfather subsequently became a member), elected by the commoners, was set up to secure the commoners' rights and the forest was also protected under the Commons Act. The remaining six thousand acres of the forest now belong to East Sussex County Council, which is responsible for its continued preservation.

C I too have my experience of the magic of the Ashdown Forest. In the early 1980s I worked for a verderer and his wife in the woods at Danehill, not far from the forest (which is actually an ancient heath). Among other things we raised pheasants and that was where I first really learnt how the countryside had been shaped for field sports. Planning a drive from one wood to the next made it very obvious to a townie like me that what I had thought of as simply clumps of trees had been planted for a purpose. I also learnt about game cover and how to plant delicious things that pheasants like, such as Good King Henry, to stop them straying. I collected squirrel tails off the keepers, bound them in bundles and sent them to Winsor & Newton for paintbrushes, and I would go up on to the forest and mooch about trying to identify different types of tree.

There used to be charcoal burners in the Sussex woods. They were grimy, blackened men living all summer long beside their hearths in primitive huts made of branches and turves as they had done for many centuries. Charcoal burning as an industry is at least five thousand years old, really taking off with the requirements for smelting copper in the Bronze Age. Traditionally, the wood was cut into lengths and carefully layered, then covered with earth and turves so that the intake of oxygen was controlled once the fire was lit. If there was too much air the wood would merely burn to ash. The charcoal burners carefully monitored the clamp for about a week until the charcoal stage had been reached. The earth covering was then withdrawn and the charcoal allowed to cool, ready for packing.

Don't mention charcoal to Johnny. When he was a little boy Johnny's father Walter took him to see the charcoal burners. He was an enchanting small boy with his mop of red-gold curls and his sparkling blue eyes and no doubt he had been scrubbed up for the occasion. Charcoal burners lived in groups with their motts (their women) and on the occasion of his visit the motts were very taken with him. Large women, probably not wearing many clothes, wanting to embrace him and saying how they would like to keep him with them would be alarming enough for any small boy, but in those days the children's books were full of stories of children kidnapped by gypsies, so poor little Johnny had nightmares for weeks. I suspect they still cross his dreams from time to time as he is not particularly fond of barbecues.

The charcoal burners took their art very seriously and different woods had different uses. Alder, for instance, was traditionally used in the making of gunpowder and is I believe still used for black powder. It was also used in cheesemaking and gave the bite to Wensleydale cheese. Charcoal was essential for smelting metal until it was replaced by coke in the eighteenth century, but it was also used in water filters and for preserving food on board ships, among other things. Sussex was a big producer of metal goods at one time and needed a lot of charcoal. Charcoal burning also produces a side product known as carbon disulphide, which is used in the artificial silk industry and as an embalming fluid. Charcoal was used as a heating source on the Continent, but this was never common in England except in East Anglia, where the strong French and Flemish influences led to the use of metal braziers for heating.

Nowadays the passion for barbecues makes charcoal a sought-after commodity and there is British charcoal, usually made from hazel, on the market. However, its modern production is less romantic and more pedestrian. It is, I learn, produced in steel drums. I get more heebie jeebies at the thought of nice modern steel furnaces than Johnny ever got from the gypsies but then I was raised on the sort of rhyme that read: 'Last night I slept in a goose feather bed with the sheets turned down so bravely, oh/But tonight I will sleep in a wild open field along with the raggle-taggle gypsies, oh.' Today's gypsies are more likely to be New Age travellers, who are a rather different kettle of fish.

When I was a young barrister I solemnly learnt that coppicing was *frutus industrialis* and the right of the tenant rather than the landlord. Trouble was, I didn't really know what coppicing was, but most of us have been in a coppice, often without knowing it. Coppicing is an early form of woodland management that was essential because trees left to their own devices grow too close together and very messily, competing for light and filling available spaces with scrub. It was commonplace until the nineteenth century and is still practised today, although to a lesser extent. To coppice a tree you cut it back to its root ball or 'stool', a little way above the forest floor, to avoid damp and infection. New shoots grow again from the stool and are rigorously pruned so that only the stongest grow straight up towards the canopy. Coppiced woods are divided into coups which are harvested at different times so that there is always growth within the wood. Depending on the soil and species, and the intended purpose of the wood, harvesting takes place at intervals of up to twenty years, and the stools may last for as long as a hundred years of repeated harvesting before they need replacing. As the growing canopy is periodically cut back, light comes in again and dormant wildflowers proliferate. Primroses and bluebells flourish and mushrooms grow in abundance.

Coppiced trees produce poles which are cut young and used for all manner of things, such as fencing stakes, depending on the wood. Nowadays coppicing is mostly done with sweet chestnuts and beeches but many other woods were coppiced and many traditional craftsmen earned their living in and from the woods. Although a bodged job is now one that has gone wrong, bodging was originally one of the woodland crafts. The word comes from a family called Bodger who came from Herefordshire, and there is still a wood there that bears their name. Bodgers made chair legs and stretchers from beech, setting up camp in the woods

Coppicing

during the summer and mass-producing their wares from the wood around them, using pole lathes that were driven by treadle power and easily constructed from materials found in the woods. Beech is a white wood which cuts like cheese when new, takes a stain very evenly and becomes very waterproof if smoked. Turned wooden bowls and plates of beech were used as crockery or for storage, and it is still used for making tubs and barrels and even clog bottoms.

Ash is a tough but flexible wood that doesn't splinter, making it ideal for implement handles and tools such as forks and rakes. Wheel rims and cart shafts, and the traditional gate hurdles used for temporary sheep enclosures, were also made from ash. Scotland still specialises in 'stooled' ash, the second or third growth from the cut-back root or stool, which is particularly good for bending for furniture, and I have at home a beautiful desk and two bookcases which I had bespoke-made from Scottish ash by Anna Karenina Fairburn.

The horse chestnut is a latecomer to the British Isles, having been introduced by that great gardener and horticulturalist John Tradescant. It is well recorded how a Dutch sailing captain gave him some conkers which were supposed to be a preventative for rheumatism. He planted these and from them came all the horse chestnuts in the country. As Lord Cecil's gardener he planted the first avenue at Theobalds, the house that James I 'acquired' from Robert Cecil.

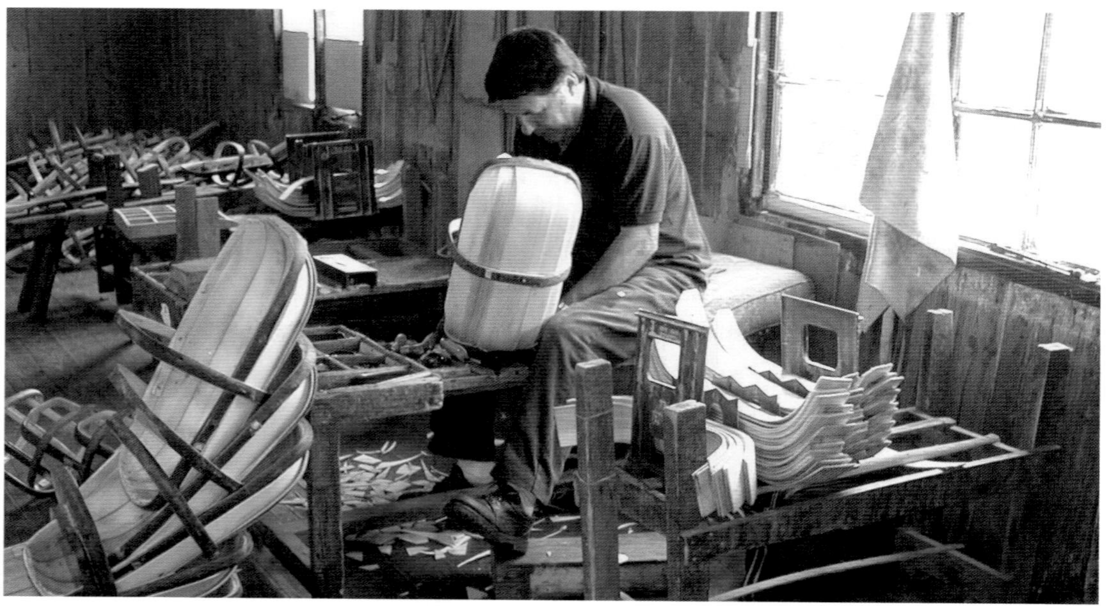

A Sussex trug for a Sussex boy

The tree is often planted for its statuesque form and its decorative candles and conkers. The unrelated sweet or Spanish chestnut is coppiced for garden furniture and stakes. As a Sussex boy Johnny always gardens with a traditional Sussex trug, a useful boat-shaped basket with a bent chestnut handle and rim to which slats of oak are nailed. First launched into the gardening world in 1851 by Thomas Smith of Herstmonceux, trugs are *de rigueur* in gardening circles: their shape is ideal for carrying cut flowers or runner beans, and dead heads and weeds get stuck less often than in basket weave.

The salix willow is native to the British Isles. It is grown along river banks to help hold up the embankment and is often pollarded. Smaller species of willow are coppiced in special withy beds, and grow so easily and fast that the beds can be cut annually. Until relatively recently, almost all produce was harvested and transported in baskets and hampers made of willow, which was the most widely used of all trees and, in a sense, the plastic of its day. Willow is a flexible and versatile material that is easy to work and can be woven into containers of all shapes and sizes. It is fairly waterproof and was used for washboards and waterwheel slats, and to make coracles (small round portable boats used for fishing) and oars. As it takes heat well, willow bowls were used for pouring hot liquids or fats into in kitchens. (I still use a willow bowl for storing my dripping.) Willow was also used for wattle and daub, the earliest form of building, where a woven wattle structure was filled in with the daub, often containing cow dung, which keeps away flies wonderfully when dry. With a floor of mud and dried blood layered and polished as glossy as any marble, you were warm, snug and bug free.

Oak is the king of the forest. There are two types of oak native to Britain: *Quercus robur*, the pedunculate oak where the leaves are stalkless but the acorns swing; and *Quercus petraea*, the sessile oak, which is the other way round, or so my father taught me. Historically oaks were not coppiced, as mature trees were needed for ship building and house construction, but they were often underplanted with coppice, a system known as coppice with standards. The Navy Commissioners kept a weather eye on most of the oak trees in the British Isles, and Charles II caused great commotion when he established large plantations of oak trees within the New Forest, but the country was glad of them when they were harvested for Nelson's navy and gave us the better ships in the Napoleonic Wars. Oak is immensely strong and heart of oak is used for ladder rungs and wheel spokes. One of the great harvests from oak trees is their bark, which is stripped and used in the tanning trade. There was an endless demand for leather, and at one time every town and large estate had its own tannery. We were lucky enough to visit one that has survived more or less intact, which you will find described in Chapter 9.

Other woods had more specialised uses. Box is a fine, close-grained wood still used by instrument makers. Elm, a hard, damp-resistant wood, was much used for coffins and fine coffers and, as it turned well, for bobbins on fish nets and bowls. Holly lacks resilience but cannot be split or easily broken and was used for tools of stress such as wedges and battens for panniers. It was illegal to use holly sticks for driving animals as the lack of resilience causes bruising. This is not an early form of animal rights but simply due to the fact that bruised meat will not take a salt cure properly and the meat may mortify. Hornbeam was used for the cogs for mill wheels, and walnut for furniture and for stocks for crossbows and guns. It is a proven fact that if a walnut tree is beaten, the wood hardens better, hence the old adage, 'A dog, a wife and a walnut tree: the more you beat them the better they be.' Yew was grown in churchyards as it is poisonous to cattle, and was the source of England's puissance since it made the long bow.

A besom fit for a witch

Besoms (witches' brooms) are made of birch twigs, and a proper sauce mousseline is never as good unless whipped with a bundle of birch twigs. Place a lattice of birch twigs at the bottom of your stew pot to stop the meat sticking. Then of course there is the bluer side of the leisure industry. The rest of the wood is less useful and is best burned: birch is the wood which gave quality to the whisky still and the unique taste to smoked haddock or herring which is lacking in today's smoking, and it remains a good source of firewood.

Trees that were to be felled for firewood used to be bled of their sap so that the wood burned more easily and with a clearer flame. In the spring the sap rises in the outer rings of the tree under the bark, which is why cutting a complete ring in the bark at this time of year will kill any tree, while cutting an incomplete ring is a good way to restrain a rather wildly growing fruit tree. In some species such as birch or maple the sap pours forth as if from a tap. Birch sap was used for making a rather potent wine and maple, of course, for maple syrup.

The crafts engendered by woodland industry were once a central part of the rural economy. There is something of a revival in traditional basket weaving. The National Museum of Scotland recently ran an exhibition of modern work and I bought a laundry basket and a log basket. The former is quite plain but the latter has different coloured willow woven into it. The advantage of these over plastic, apart from the obvious visual one, is that they are very resilient and won't crack easily. Another craft that remains is the making of hurdles. These are panels of woven wood (usually hazel rods) which are now used mainly as fencing but once had widespread uses in the building industry and in agriculture, when animals were hurdled for protection or for manuring the fields. The dead and wounded were carried home from battle or the hunting field on a hurdle, which was as pliant as a cloth stretcher but less likely to rip. Itinerant woodland workers made use of every part of the woodland tree, and even the nettles that grew in the open spaces were beaten into flax and used for clothing. German army shirts in the First World War were of nettle flax. I have a friend whose grandfather came from Russia and set up a basket weaving factory in the East End of London (in the 1890s everything was carted in hampers). In the Second World War he sold containers to the War Office to drop munitions to resistance groups as they were flexible and didn't show up on radar.

Today plastic has replaced most of the woodland products, to no ecological advantage.

J In the 1960s, 1970s and into the mid-1980s, successive governments were obsessed with the idea that Britain had to be self-supporting in the event of another war. This was a laudable aim when the horrors of U-boats and rationing were still vivid in people's minds. Maximisation of land usage was instigated. Large areas of marshy land were drained and hedgerows bulldozed out to create prairie farms, destroying the habitat of millions of little animals and insects. Headlands were vigorously sprayed and the chemicals leaching into the rivers virtually killed off otters. Run-off from agricultural fertilisers and acid rain from massive blocks of forestry seriously reduced salmon stocks on our valuable game rivers. Traditional family farms with their mixed agriculture were replaced by monoculture. Before long we were overproducing and terrible damage had been done to the landscape in many parts of the country.

The decision to encourage the planting of conifers is just one example. Between the wars there were some commercial conifer plantings for paper, pit props and cheap building materials but these were tiny compared to the postwar horrors. 'Large scale systematic forestry,' said a report in the late 1940s, 'is necessary for the safety and welfare of Britain.' Planting on the scale anticipated by some megalomaniac sylviculturist in the post-war Ministry of Agriculture would provide massive reserves of timber in an emergency. It would bring our land, particularly the poorer parts that really hadn't been pulling their weight, into full and valuable production. Isolated communities would be revitalised and the cinema, that essential recreation for the weary Forestry Commission worker, brought to remote rural areas. Once it

Conifer planting in Kielder Forest

was up and running, timber production would be a great national industry. Just what was needed to put Britain back on the map and make her the envy of the rest of the world.

The awful thing is that the idea captured government imagination and actually took place. It was, in my opinion, the greatest act of vandalism in the history of these islands. Conifer planting on a gigantic scale was soon under way in Northumberland, Snowdonia and the Highlands. Kielder Forest, covering a vast area of the lovely Cheviot Hills, is the biggest manmade forest in Europe. It has displaced farming communities and replaced them with a migrant workforce. The degree of spoliation of our upland beauty spots in Wales, Scotland and its islands, and northern England is beyond belief. The great black plantation blocks cover tens of thousands of acres, and are so closely planted that they support no wildlife other than foxes and birds of prey. Ground-nesting birds are rarely seen in the vicinity of big areas of forestry planting – the lack of birdlife on the once famous and productive Welsh grouse moors is a tragic example.

In a world where modern farming practices were threatening the very existence of game species, the forerunners of the present Game Conservancy Trust (GCT) were among the pioneers of wildlife habitat conservation. Starting in the 1920s when disease was threatening the indigenous grey partridge, their painstaking work has helped to save much of our wild bird population from extinction. As early as the 1960s, the GCT with others including the then Nature Conservancy were largely responsible for persuading the Ministry of Agriculture to ban the use of Dieldrin, Aldron and Heptachlor – chemicals that killed the plants and insects upon which the bird population depends – in sheep dips and for dressing spring corn. As our towns expand and more of the countryside disappears, conservation is of increasing national importance. The GCT continues to be one of the leaders in the environmental field with its scientific research, and all the field sports organisations are involved, including the British Association for Shooting and Conservation, the Countryside Alliance and the Masters of Hounds Association. Purdey, the London gunmakers, present an annual award to shoots both large and small, to demonstrate that 'shooting works for conservation' by encouraging good woodland management.

A classic example of this is a small shoot in a wood on the outskirts of Reading, in a built-up area where pressure on wildlife from walkers, dogs, trespassers, fly-tipping and building is enormous. Like all countrymen, the owner has a love of tree planting and scrupulously maintains his woodlands. His existing hedges are kept trimmed and tidy, and new ones are planted. These act as corridors of safety from predators for small birds and animals. Headlands are kept wide to provide feed for roe deer, to a level where grazing pressure will not damage young saplings. The owner has created an ideal habitat for game birds and, just as importantly, established an oasis for wildlife in a sea of houses.

Hedge laying

Hunting has contributed to the way the landscape has been fashioned for more than three hundred years, and in today's conservation-sensitive environment the hunts' role in the management of woodland has an even greater significance. There are 312 registered hound packs in the British Isles, covering 150,000 square miles of hunting country. As well as owning 6,500 acres of covert and over 1,500 acres of paddocking, they are also involved in the thousands of acres of woodland in the areas over which they hunt. Not least, they provide the incentive for farmers and landowners to maintain old hedges and plant new ones. Stockproof hedgerows are labour-intensive to keep in good condition and they exist in hunting countries largely because of their value in providing jumps for the mounted field. They also provide habitats for a wide range of flora and fauna and this is particularly important when seen in the light of the miles of hedgerows that were destroyed during the second half of the twentieth century. In the 1990s, 2,500 miles of hedging was being lost each year. Many hunts, like the

Cottesmore in Leicestershire and the Ashford Valley in Kent support hedge-laying societies and run annual competitions.

There are often woodlands in hunting countries that are designated 'ancient', and hunts, like any other responsible modern landlord, have entered into agreements with various heritage bodies to manage Sites of Special Scientific Interest (SSSI). The Belvoir and the Woodland Pytchley collaborate with English Heritage, and the Puckeridge raised funds back in the 1970s to buy Hormead Park Wood in Hertfordshire when it was about to be felled for agricultural conversion. Today it is a vitally important SSSI supporting the rare oxlip and containing the last fragments of Ermine Street, once a famous Roman thoroughfare. The Sinnington manage an area of gorse in West Yorkshire which supports one of the few colonies remaining in eastern England of the pearl-bordered fritillary butterfly and the rare dog violets on which their caterpillars feed. Every hunt is involved in maintaining old coverts and planting new ones.

The Portman, where Hugo Busby has been Master and Huntsman for the last six seasons, is a typical example of the role hunting plays in conserving wildlife and its habitat. The Portman country is in that lovely part of Dorset from Shaftesbury to Wimborne and across from Cranborne to Milton Abbas. Like other masters, Hugo has developed a close working relationship with local conservation bodies such as the National Trust, the Williams Trust, English Nature, the Woodland Trust, the Dorset Wildlife Trust and, where they have woodland, the Forestry Commission. The Portman hill country is mostly open with light plough, downland and large woodland. The vale is well fenced with good thorn hedging and ditches. Smashing galloping country. When not involved in hunting, Hugo and his terrierman, Nick Stevens, who is a passionate woodsman, are actively engaged every year planting new woodland and managing established coverts. In the past year the hunt has cut and laid seventeen hedges and organises an annual hedge-laying competition. For their work the Portman won the Regional Conservation Award presented by the MFHA in conjunction with *Country Illustrated*.

Organised covert shooting changed very little during the twentieth century, except in its importance as a form of income to landowners. Agricultural returns on many estates now barely cover upkeep. Without shooting revenues many would be bankrupt. Shooting brings about £100 million into the Scottish economy annually, with obvious benefits to local employment and the rural infrastructure, including the support of peripheral industries such as the manufacture of specialised seed mixes for wild birds and game feed. Scotland's heather-carpeted landscape is largely maintained by sporting revenues. If these went, the vista that is so attractive to tourists would revert to scrub and heathland or have to be managed at vast cost to the taxpayer.

The appearance of the countryside changes as hedges are replanted

Building on the role farmers have always played in caring for the countryside, there are now government incentives to repair some of the damage caused by their previous encouragement of overproduction. We are given financial assistance towards management that goes beyond normal good agricultural practice. These schemes cover a wide range of important issues. Farmers are now encouraged to manage grassland for the benefit of birds by creating species-rich grasses and keeping stock off during the nesting period. Sensitive management of wetlands, water margins, flood plains and beetle banks creates biodiversity and encourages wildfowl habitat. Moorland management and stock reduction to encourage suppressed heather and other moorland vegetation provides an environment for migratory ground-nesting birds. There is financial assistance for works such as the building and restoration of stone dykes (and there are thousands of yards of those on the farm), and where there were once grants for grubbing out hedges, there are now grants for replanting them. The preservation of the British landscape has been left in the hands of sporting farmers and landowners for too long. It was high time that government played a part in redressing the ills it has helped to create.

One of the grant-aided schemes that is of particular interest to me is the planting of broadwood trees. Planting small areas of woodland is part of my existing Countryside Premium Scheme. Larger areas on the lower end of the farm will be planted with the aid of farm woodland initiatives run by the Forestry Authority. There is no doubt that support for upland farming will gradually shift from rearing livestock to enhancing landscape, and as hardwood planting grows up, the scenery of Britain will change yet again.

CHAPTER FOUR

THE MOST NOBLE BEAST

Just before Christmas, Clarissa and I were staying overnight at the Castle Hotel in Taunton on our way down to the West Country when we met Michael Scott, the son of one of the Joint Masters of the Devon and Somerset Staghounds. I used to come down to Exmoor with my parents and sister for the autumn stag hunting in the 1960s, staying at the Crown in Exford for three weeks every August before going back to school. Later on, when I worked in London, I would escape to the wide open spaces of this lovely part of England for a day's hind hunting in the winter. I was reminiscing with him about the moor and the people that I had known then when he kindly suggested we had a day with them. 'We can easily mount you,' he offered, 'but unfortunately we don't allow quads. Clarissa could get a ride in one of the Land Rovers.' In the warm glow of the moment and the flood of happy memories released by this prospect, I hardly noticed Clarissa's lack of enthusiasm.

The following day we drove across to Newmarket for Greyhound 2000, a millennium celebration of the coursing dog and the first 128-

dog stake to be run for a hundred years. From time to time I thought that Clarissa's usual ebullience was tempered by moments of pensive introspection. After we got back from Newmarket I was away goose shooting on the Tay for a few days with my son Sam. When I telephoned Clarissa on my return, her conversation was punctuated by stentorian grunts, little moans and gasps for breath. In the background I could hear a peculiar thumping sound. Must have got company, I thought, hurriedly ringing off.

The next time we had dinner together I noticed that Clarrie's normal aperitif, a lemonade with ice, no slice, was replaced by mineral water. I raised a quizzical eyebrow at this departure from the norm. 'Given up sugary drinks. Must think of the horse,' she murmured nonchalantly by way of explanation. 'Horse? What's all this about a horse?' I wanted to know. 'Bugger following in a Land Rover,' she told me, with that all too familiar look. 'I'm going to ride again. Can't think why I gave it up. Need to tone up the muscles, so I'm exercising every morning. Found this machine in the shed someone gave me years ago. A bit rusty but it seems to work. That's what I was doing when you rang up the other day. I rise to the trot on a chair as well. If I keep it up I should be ready by next season.'

One of the things I love about Clarissa is her determination to have a go, regardless of the possible consequences. Last year, only weeks after major surgery, she trudged for miles across the Norfolk marshes on a pitch dark January morning to watch the migratory geese rising from their shore roosts and experience the thrill of wildfowling, to say nothing of careering over the Cheviots after the Border hounds on a quad. Taking up riding again was bordering on martyrdom, but one great paradox of the attempts to make controlling vermin with dogs a criminal offence has been a massive increase in the support of hunting. All sorts of people who have never hunted before are turning out to see what it's all about and many who had stopped hunting have started once more.

'Right,' I said, striking when the iron was hot. 'The sooner we find you something to ride, the sooner you'll get fit.' The search for a suitable horse was on.

C Painfully I lay aside the pretty little hunting crop from Pentland whips that Johnny has given me for my birthday and dismount my chair. Yes, I did say chair: for ten minutes every morning I post to the trot on a chair. The whip doesn't make the chair go any faster but it consoles me.

It is over twenty years since I was last on a horse, but my great heroine Mrs V. D. S. Williams, the Olympic gold medallist and dressage expert, never set foot in a stirrup until she was fifty. As a child I was never more than competent and heavens knows what I will be now, but my grandmother, my mother and my sister Heather all rode side-saddle superbly. I remember my mother telling me when I went back to school that posting on a chair was the only way to keep the riding muscles fit. Religiously amidst the mirth of my friends I followed her advice and now, despite hoots from Johnny, I am returned to the discipline. Johnny threatens to sell the chair for a fortune for charity but I ignore him stoically.

Riding side-saddle

It would be strange if, in a family with so much Irish blood, horses weren't part of my earliest memories. I can remember my mother reading me tales of Cuchulain, the hound of Ulster, and his chariot horse, the grey of Macha. I can see myself now, propped up in bed with the tears streaming down my cheeks, as she read the sad story of Cuchulain's tragic death and his brave horse's heroic defence of his master. Years later I came to read Homer and was immediately struck by how alike the Celtic Irish and the Greek civilisations were. Homer was writing about the siege of Troy around 800 BC while the Red Rose kings of pre-Christian Ireland were some four hundred years later but the description of Achilles' chariot horses could be from Irish mythology. And of course they raced, albeit chariots, but the prize was to the swift.

Racing was in my blood and my nurturing. My father, who went to the Great War as a horse gunner, rode only adequately but he loved his racing. At the time of those two great horses Mill Reef and Brigadier Gerard, he had a running double which made him a great deal of money and was mentioned frequently in the newspapers. My mother's father had gone to the Boer War in the Queensland Mounted Light Infantry (truly there was such a regiment). On his return home to Australia, he started one of the first horsebreeding farms in the Hunter

Valley, where they had only just removed the prickly pear. He bred cavalry remounts. After his death, my grandmother and uncle transformed it into a racing stud. My uncle became chairman of the Turf Club in Singapore and was on its committee in Australia. When I was only four, my grandmother's chestnut colt Blue Lamp, trained by Reg Day and ridden by Scobie Breasley, won the New Stakes at Royal Ascot. It was a proud moment and the bronze stood on my mother's mantelpiece for as long as I can remember.

My grandmother was a superb horsewoman. Most pictures of her are in breeches and boots, usually without her side-saddle apron. From the age of thirteen, she lived her life in Australia and the Far East. She went pigsticking side-saddle, drove a four-in-hand, and followed the bush packs after dingoes. When her daughter, my mother, married and came to live in England in 1928, they shipped her favourite horse from Singapore. She too was a fine horsewoman and hunted side-saddle with great panache.

My mother had a lifetime's fascination with buying horses. She raced steeplechasers without great success, her best being her beloved Scots Prince, who was third in the Irish National. From time to time I was called on to exercise these giants, who had no mouth and went from a walk to a gallop with nothing in between. She persuaded Arthur Budgett, who had bred two Derby winners, Morston and Blakeney, out of his old mare Windmill Girl, to sell us the last colt, which had been born too late to race in Europe. Above Water was shipped out to Australia, but never acclimatised in time to run there either. However, he did become leading sire of two-year-olds in the southern hemisphere. I grew up going to race meetings and can remember accompanying my mother to Cheltenham for the Irish meeting in the days before there were televisions in the bars. My mother sent me outside with her binoculars to tell her when the horses were coming round the top turn. It was freezing cold and snowing and I stood there peering into the murk, trembling with excitement and cold.

Men have raced horses since the dawn of time. The first records come from Homer. Initially races in horse-drawn chariots were, like all athletic events, attached to funerals. Funeral games drew people from all over Greece in peacetime, and in time of war the death of a hero caused a lull in the proceedings so that all might attend. All who have read Homer (and if you haven't you must) cannot fail to have been gripped by the description of the chariot race held to commemorate the death of Patroclus, Achilles' lover. Spectating must have been difficult, as most of the horses were dun-coloured. The only other colourings mentioned are 'phoenix', interpreted as chestnut, and the 'fair-maned' team of Meriones, which must have been palaminos. Stallions and mares were both entered and there was even one mixed team, although this may be poetic licence since it would have led to some hair-raising moments. It is a lengthy descriptive passage well worth the reading. In ancient Greece, as in every period of history since, horse racing was a game for the rich. Alcibiades, the tyrant of Athens who died in 404 BC, is noted as the private owner who won the most prizes while the immensely rich Philip II of Macedon, father of Alexander the Great, was the Sheikh Mohammed of his day.

Advice on breeding, rearing and training has come down to us from the Scythians, the Parthians, the Indians and the Romans, and much of it is still practised today. Why, you may ask, were they racing chariots only, for there were no ridden races. The answer is that they were all waiting for that great invention, the stirrup. Without stirrups, it is difficult to ride at a gallop for any length of time. The first description of a mounted race comes to us in Alfred the Great's preface to a translation of the geography book of Orosius. It refers to the practice in Estonia (which was, by the way, the only western European country to adopt the Mongol-Tartar drink of fermented mares' milk, which they drank in preference to ale):

> There is a custom with the Estonians, that when a man is dead, he lies, in his house, unburnt with his kindred and friends a month – sometimes two... All the while the body is within, there must be drinking and sports to the day, on which he is burned.
>
> Then, the same day, when they wish to bear him to the pile, they divide his property, which is left after the drinking and sports, into five or six parts, sometimes into more, as the amount of his property may be. Then, they lay the largest part of it within one mile from the town, then another, then the third, till it is all laid, within the one mile; and the least part shall be nearest the town in which the dead man lies. All the men, who have the swiftest horses in the land, shall then be assembled, about five or six miles from the property. Then they all run towards the property; and the man, who has the swiftest horse, comes to the first and the largest part, and so each after the other, til it is all taken: and he takes the least part, who runs to the property nearest the town. Then each rides away with the property, and may keep it all; and, therefore, swift horses are there uncommonly dear.
>
> Alfred, *Whole Works: Orosius Book I*

Poor Alfred kept importing horses to build up the royal studs so as to defeat the Danes but the British kept eating them. Finally, in despair, he got the Archbishop of Canterbury to issue an anathema against the eating of horse flesh, which is probably why we alone among our continental neighbours don't eat it.

The Church has long disapproved of racing, deeming it pagan, and Tertullian, one of the earliest theologians, did his best to get it banned altogether but to no avail. Horse racing in Britain really began with the Stuarts, all of whom were magnificent horsemen. Mary, Queen of Scots' fantastic ride across Scotland when heavily pregnant shows the gene line. James VI and I, though very bandy-legged, was a superlative huntsman and horseman and it was he who first imported Arab and Turkish blood into the breeding lines. His grandson Charles II carried

Godolphin Arabian

on the good work after he was restored to the throne and re-established the Royal Stud, together with the first fixed racecourse, at Newmarket, where they have remained ever since.

All British racehorses are supposedly descended from three sires: the Byerley Turk, the Darley Arabian and the Godolphin Arabian. The story of the Godolphin Arabian is the stuff of fairy tales, but thought to be true. The second Lord Godolphin was a wealthy Cornishman whose family had made a fortune from silver and tin in the seventeenth century. He was a noted breeder and his stallion, Hobgoblin, was the best in the land. Pictures show it as a large, old-fashioned horse, better suited to breeding hunters. The Bey of Tunis had given four horses to the King of France, who didn't really know what to do with them as they were light Arab stock, so he gave them away. How one of them came to be drawing a water cart in Paris has never been explained but it was spotted by Lord Godolphin's agent, who bought it out of the shafts. He sent it to Hougemount, the Godolphin stud, where the stud manager viewed it with scorn and used it as a teaser to test the mares that were brought to Hobgoblin. The Arab became enraged, killed Hobgoblin, covered the mare and the progeny was the Godolphin Arabian. Lord Godolphin had the courage to race this new lightweight at Newmarket, where it romped home.

Racing is full of such stories, which is one reason why it is so addictive and attracts such huge crowds. It is not just the gambling or the thrill of the race but the incalculable romance. Think of Red Rum, three times Grand National winner, who was kept in a stable little better than a shed and trained on the sands; Oxo, bought for £60, to save it from going for horsemeat; and Shergar, thought to have been killed by the IRA. The list is endless.

But I digress. As Johnny says, I won't need a blood horse. A nice quiet cob will do me very well. 'Anything really,' he adds, 'that is up to weight.'

J In our search for a suitable horse for Clarissa, weight, I fancy, will be an important consideration. Still, as I pointed out to her, keeping well out of range, a troop horse in the Heavies was expected to carry twenty stone. What we needed was described by the Colonel Commandant of the 12th Light Dragoons in 1811. The ideal mount, he said, should be 'active and fully master of seventeen stone'. Just in case the chair and exercise machine fail us. 'Remember, stout and good limbs – stout backs – good feet – open in the counter – good shoulders and well up before. Deep chested and not light carcassed, not too heavy in the hind quarters, but strong in the gammon and open between the jaws.' Sounds perfect.

My father's regiment, the 1st Royal Dragoons, were mounted on horses exactly the same as these when he joined the equitation course at the army school at Weedon in 1939, straight from Cambridge. It seems incredible that he was trained as a cavalryman for the first year of the war – I still have his manual of mounted sword drill – until the Royals became mechanised in 1940. Except for this short absence during the war, my father was one of those lucky people who were able to devote their entire lives to horses: their breeding and welfare, and the promotion of riding through the Pony Club, hunting and hunter trials. He had his first pony at the age of five and was breeding Connemaras when he died aged seventy-four, having finally given up riding only a few years before.

Immediately after the war, he bought several hunters off the Peats, well-known horse dealers whose yard was over near Tunbridge Wells. In the mid-1950s he started breeding, following methods that had been tried and tested over two centuries. Two Welsh cob brood mares were added to the hunters already in stables. These were crossed with thoroughbred stallions and their progeny crossed again to thoroughbreds to produce beautiful lightweight hunters. Some went on to become eventers, under the gentle schooling of Joyce Cartwright, assisted by Jenny Baker, both of whom helped my father for years. They shared with him what is now called 'whispering ability' but used to be known simply as 'having a way with horses'.

A lightweight hunter, to carry up to 13 stone 7 pounds and standing 16 hands (a hand being 4 inches), with plenty of quality, is a relatively easy target to achieve. A middleweight hunter to carry under 14 stone 7 pounds and a 17-hand heavy hunter over that weight are both less easy to breed successfully. If a horse is to carry weight, the necessary introduction of common blood is made at the expense of quality. My father rode over 15 stone and his ultimate goal was to breed for himself what he considered to be the perfect heavy hunter.

The hunter is a type rather than a breed, of which the Leicestershire horse – one that can be hunted in the shires – is regarded as the definitive article by hunting people. He needs to be able to follow hounds over big fast country, carry weight and stay. To possess both power and speed, a horse requires a lot of thoroughbred blood, and with blood goes looks.

There is a huge range of hunters, bred to suit different hunting countries. A glance through *Baily's Hunting Directory* will tell you what is likely to suit and where. A big galloping Leicestershire jumper isn't going to be much use on the northern hills with the Border, the College Valley or the North Tyne where a three-quarter-bred or clever hill pony is needed. You would need a good, breedy jumper to cope with the Shropshire clay, woodland and trappy obstacles expected in the Wheatland country, but less blood and more sense when you're up on the Devon moors with the Lamerton, and a short-legged, active, clever sort to handle the rocky dingles and wet hill going with the Goathland in North Yorkshire. The range covers everything from a high-class horse to the old-fashioned 'ride and drive' cob like my beloved Badger on whom I spent many happy days as a boy.

I have six oil paintings of the horses that belonged to my grandparents just before the war, painted by the equestrian artist E. M. Hollams on her favourite material, wooden teachest tops. Three are bays which my grandfather rode, big horses standing 17 hands or so. The others are smaller and finer, 16 hands or a little over, on which Grandmother rode side-saddle. They are classic examples of middleweight and lightweight hunters.

They stand poised on sound, open feet showing plenty of horn, tacked up and ready to go, with their long necks stretching forward and their bright intelligent eyes searching the distance. They possess substance and quality. Their withers are well developed and strong, with broad, level, muscular backs. One of the bays shows the characteristic little arch at the loins that suggests a first-rate fencer. Their shoulders are long and sloping, with just a hint of shoulder blade showing through the skin. Their loins are strong and the ribs well hooped, yet they stand over plenty of ground. Their quarters are deep and powerful, with tails well set on long muscular thighs, the second thigh noticeably well developed, running into large clean hocks. They are the culmination of centuries of careful breeding which began in the seventeenth century.

In Tudor times, a gentleman's stable would have included a variety of horses and ponies, used for different purposes, but breeding was fairly haphazard in the sixteenth century. A gentleman was required by law to keep a courser, or heavy war horse. This would have been not unlike a palfrey, the medieval knight's riding horse, and was a cross between the 'great' horse he used in battle and a Barb. Before Arabs were imported in any quantity in the seventeenth century, Barbs were the great improvers. Similar to the Arab but lacking their vital spark, these north African horses were imported to Europe when the Moors invaded Spain

Johnny's grandmother's hunter, Grey Dawn

and used extensively across Europe. The Tudor gentleman would also have had hunting geldings (cobby sorts, similar to but more active than a courser) for the laborious woodland hunting of the time; a hobby or pad (a native breed crossed to a Barb) with the Barb's ambling gait; some packhorses; and a stalking horse or two for shooting. If he was really flush with cash, he might even have had a team of big Flemish draughts, descendants of the great horse, to pull his lumbering coach.

In 1576, the Italian Prospero D'Osma drew attention to the idea of selective breeding in a report on the condition of the Royal Stud commissioned by the Earl of Leicester. His suggestions were followed, and improvements to breeding began to stabilise at the beginning of the seventeenth century. A stud book was established in 1605, and north African and Barb stallions, chosen for their absolute excellence, docility, soundness, speed and stamina, were carefully selected and crossed on to the little racing Galloway. This cross, bred for racing, was the beginning of what was to become the thoroughbred.

Cromwell accelerated the spread of quality in horse breeding by breaking up many private stables for his cavalry remounts and dispersing some of the finest breeding stock around the country. Not even the Royal Stud at Tutbury was spared. Quality breeding was no longer localised to particular studs or exclusive to the nobility.

With the return of Charles II from exile and the glorious age of the Restoration, racing began again with all the pent-up vigour that had been smothered by the puritanism of the Commonwealth. New racecourses sprang up all over the country and a fresh wave of eastern horses from Syria, Turkey and the Lebanon were imported after Sir John Fenwick, Master of the Horse, returned from a buying expedition to the Levant. Racing provided the opportunity for royalty, the nobility and the squirearchy to test the advances in their development of the thoroughbred. Of all the magnificent stallions that came into the country from the east at the end of the seventeenth century and the beginning of the eighteenth, three in particular are recognised as being the foundation stock of the British racehorse: the Byerley Turk, imported by Captain Byerley in 1689; the Darley Arabian, brought over to Mr Darley's stud in 1704; and Lord Godolphin's Arab of 1728, already mentioned by Clarissa.

Gradually, as the seventeenth century moved into the eighteenth, the appalling roads began to improve, creating the need for different types of horse. Light draught geldings from Holland appeared between the shafts of smart town turnouts, replacing the heavy Flemish horses and lumbering, ungainly coaches. Rapid advances in husbandry and stock breeding meant produce needed to be moved quickly, particularly to London. The first toll road was licensed by statute late in the seventeenth century. By the end of the first quarter of the eighteenth century, turnpike roads were widespread throughout much of England. At last people were able to get about in relative comfort and speed. Those that could afford it revelled in the novelty. As the countryside opened up, the use of eastern stallions and the nascent thoroughbreds was extended by crossing them with Dutch draughts, indigenous cobby native breeds and packhorses to create fast, light carthorses (or vanners).

Hunting as we know it today is a product of the Agricultural and Industrial Revolutions. As woodland was felled on a massive scale for fuel, destroying game cover, the old ponderous woodland hunting changed. Georgian hunters were developed in response. A horse now needed to be fast but able to gallop well within himself to go the sometimes considerable distances involved in following hounds across the changed landscape. He had to be capable of jumping on in any circumstances and needed to be robust, with strong back, deep well-ribbed frame, good loins, plenty of bone and sound open feet. The thoroughbred's true riding action, dependent on the shape and freedom of the shoulder, was essential. For a long active day in the saddle the action had to be free, easy and low, the stride long and powerful. The vanner or light draught provided size, bone, feet and common sense, but its short, jerky action and bent knees would have been an intolerable ride. A real bum-stripper. The thoroughbred cross with the vanner brought speed, comfort and quality, and is exactly the same as today's hunter.

It is hard now to appreciate the sheer scale of horse breeding in the country during the eighteenth and nineteenth centuries. It probably reached its zenith in the 1850s and gradually dropped away when the horse lost its supremacy as a means of transport to the railways and then the motor car. Breeding was a form of diversification on almost all farms in the eighteenth century. Every permutation of harness horse was needed, from the heavier Dutch type of draught horse through carriage horses to the rangier trotters which eventually standardised into the hackney, the supreme light harness horse. The enormous demand for middleweight hunter-type cavalry remounts helped fuel those heady days of horse breeding. Packhorses, ponies and pads – the Tudor gentleman's riding horse, noted for its limitless stamina, amenable temperament and ambling gait – were all still in demand. Wherever speed and quality was needed, thoroughbred stallions were used.

The late eighteenth century was the golden age of carriage driving, with mail coaches covering distances between towns at what were then considered phenomenal speeds. During that period of competitive breeding, a horse emerged among all others as the principal coach horse. This was the tall, elegant Yorkshire coach horse, bred by crossing a strong thoroughbred with the Cleveland bay.

The Cleveland bay originated in the north-east, where in the Middle Ages the monks were the main horse breeders. Its ancestor was a sturdy packhorse known as the Chapman which was used to carry goods between the monasteries as well as to transport coal, iron ore and alum from the Yorkshire moors down to the coast. Fish and other produce were brought back on the return journey. Fortuitously, Whitby was one of the ports through which Barb stallions were imported during the seventeenth century. Before being moved to other parts of the country, these were used to cover Chapman mares. As feeding improved, the progeny of this cross developed into powerful vanners and light draught horses, noted for boldness and honesty, which became known as Cleveland bays. At one time, anyone aspiring to a smart turnout had matched pairs and teams bred from these magnificent horses. In 1879 the poet Sir J. Paul immortalised the breed in verse: 'All things that live have parallel save one;/The Cleveland bay horse, he alone has none!' Clevelands were exported all over the world and many continental warmbloods – Gelderlanders, Oldenburgs, Holsteins, Hanoverians, Russian Vladimirs and Danish Schienswigs – can claim Cleveland blood in their make-up.

The tractor and motor lorry almost did for the Cleveland. By the 1960s they had dwindled away to only a handful of mares and nine registered stallions. Arguably the best of these, Mulgrave Supreme, was purchased by HM the Queen to save it being exported to America. This has preserved the quality of the breed in its country of origin, and Cleveland bays are still used as carriage horses in the Royal Mews.

My father's two great passions at Cambridge, apart from foxhunting, were beagling and driving. He once drove a six-in-hand down the main street in Cambridge, something which was illegal even then, and was deeply disappointed when a rozzer on traffic duty didn't bat an eyelid. With his longstanding love of coaching, it is hardly surprising that he applied for a nomination from the Crown Equerry when Mulgrave Supreme became available. I still have a spare application form and the stallion's details: Mulgrave Supreme, owned by HM the Queen. By Cholderton Minstral out of Mulgrave Rose. 'This dark bay horse stands 17 hands. He has been in harness and under saddle.' By using this stallion and, later on, others of the same breed, my father achieved his lifetime ambition of breeding his ideal heavy hunter.

One of his horses would have been up to weight for Clarissa, but with too much thoroughbred blood and more height than I think she could cope with at this stage. Once, we might well have found what we were looking for at one of the many horse fairs that proliferated up and down the country during the eighteenth and nineteenth centuries. Such was the universal interest in improving breeding that many a sporting landlord allowed his prize stallions to be used by his tenantry on their mares. Sportsmen looking for a horse were able to buy their hunters direct from farmers with established reputations, or from one of the horse fairs. Horncastle in Lincolnshire was among the most important and Pembridge in Herefordshire was internationally famous for saddle horses, hunters, pads and racers.

In London there were sales for the man about town at Beevor's, Aldridge's, the Barbican, Sadler's and Tattersall's, with all the noise, drama and excitement of Regency England. Ostlers trotting the lots back and forth in front of a hoarse, purple-faced auctioneer. The swells and the dandies, insouciant bucks and Corinthians, rubbing shoulders with grooms, horse dealers, coachmen and jockeys. The farmers and fat graziers, pimps and crimpers. Whores, loungers, pickpockets and ragged urchins, street vendors and entertainers. Leviathans of the turf and wiry gypsies deep in conversation on a common topic and shared passion – horses and horse breeding.

Horse sales, where hunters could be bought, continued in popularity up until the Second World War. At Warner Shepard and Wade's yard in Leicester, many of the best Midland horses could be found and consequently the highest prices paid. Northern hunters changed hands at Doncaster and York Repositories, and down in the West Country, many of the hirelings for hunting on Exmoor passed through Colling's at Exeter. Every Monday between the end of the hunting season and the beginning of August, 11 o'clock sharp at Tattersall's, hundreds of hunters were sold in their famous premises on Hyde Park Corner.

Today, only a few horse sales remain. The only weekly horse market in London is held at Southall. Set in a predominantly Asian community, it seems strangely out of place. Skewbald and piebald gypsy cobs, Welsh ponies and a mixed collection of riding horses are put through

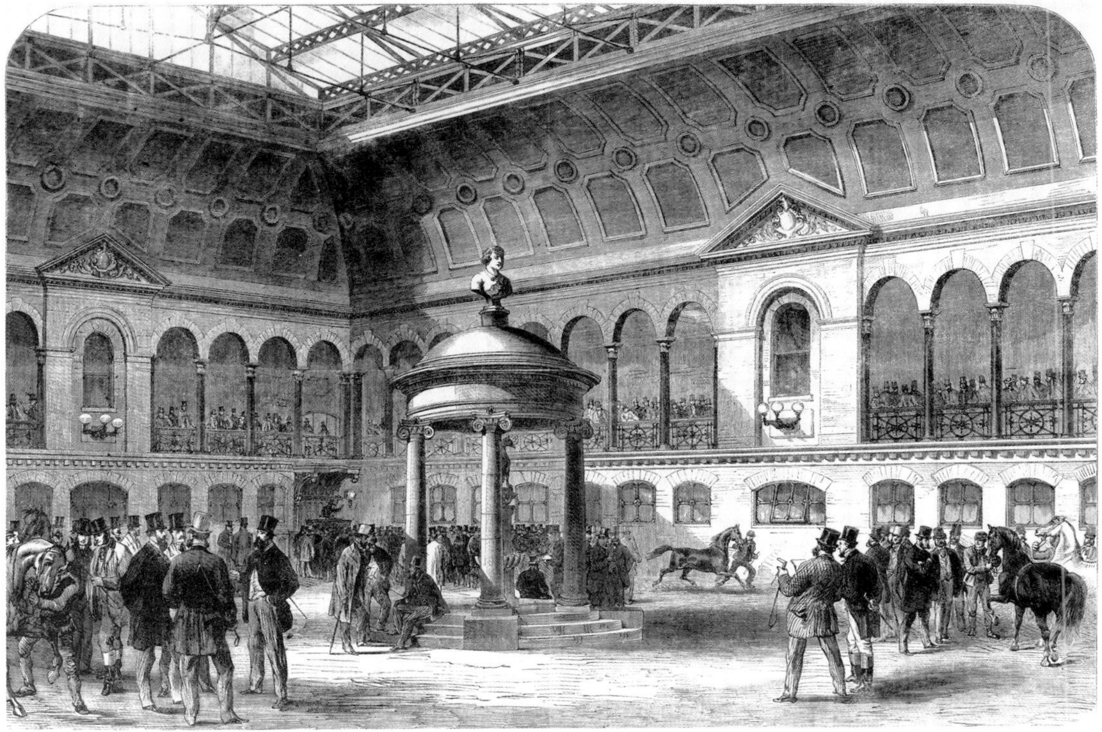

Tattersall's

their paces, with stalls selling tack, riding boots and horse nuts next to shops offering Asian produce, brilliant cloth and gaudy jewellery. Stately Asian women in flowing saris undulate past leathery old men in shirtsleeves and braces. Lost in a gentler age, these old horsemen seem oblivious to the London traffic roaring past.

Thimbleby and Shorland at Reading have monthly horse sales and occasional specialist ones for hackney horses, Shetland ponies and heavy horses. They also have four international sales each year for superb antique horse-drawn vehicles – gigs, dog carts, broughams and landaus with their harness – plus the Midlands carriage sale, reflecting the increasing popularity in driving. Brightwell's in Hereford still have a sale for hunters in July.

A flavour of pre-Victorian riotous indiscipline endures at the gypsy horse fairs. Appleby is the most famous of these great annual get-togethers, now sadly degenerating into a tourist spectacle monopolised by New Age travellers. But there are many more, unadvertised outside the horse-trading fraternity, at places like Lee Gap, Bridgwater, Boroughbridge and Yarm, where the coloured ponies are flashed up and down and the spectacularly unnerving harness races thrill spectators, among rumours of less legal entertainment – cock fighting and bare-knuckle boxing. Many of these fairs owe their continued existence to ancient royal charters,

The original Mr Tattersall in action

much to the chagrin of some local councils, who would be happier to see them closed down.

The community association at Brigg has been more enlightened in its attitude to the horse fair, granted under a charter from Henry III in 1235. Instead of trying to discourage the gypsy horse dealers, they have turned the occasion into an enormously popular attraction with funfairs, jazz bands, craft stalls, fortune tellers, street entertainers, bouncy castles and even a circus – a modern version of what it must have been like in Georgian times. There are fewer horses, of course, and the swells and dandies are missing, but I dare say if one looked hard enough there would be the odd whore and a pickpocket or two. Some things never change.

Where would one go nowadays to buy a horse off the peg, as it were, for someone wanting to take up hunting again? There is no shortage of them advertised in equestrian magazines like the *Horse and Hound* and you only have to mention you are looking for a hunter to be overwhelmed with advice and offers. Choice has to boil down to previous experience, weight, the type of country one hopes to hunt in and how often. If Clarissa wanted to set her cap and purse high and hunt with a shire pack, the person to go to would be Barbara Rich, an old friend of my Uncle Barry and Aunt Tor in Rutland.

Barbara has been buying horses in Ireland for more than fifty years. Many of her holidays were spent there as a schoolgirl, and she was fascinated by the turnover of ponies among her contemporaries and of hunters among their parents. In England people tended to hang on to what they had bought, whereas in Ireland dealing seemed to be a way of life. Barbara bought her first horse in Ireland when she was seventeen. A five-year-old liver chestnut mare for which she paid £70, it was shipped over to Liverpool and in due course arrived by train in Melton Mowbray. Barbara schooled the mare on and hunted it for a season in Leicestershire, selling it to Sir Derek Greenaway, Master of the Old Surrey and Burstow, who bought it for his Huntsman Jack Champion, for £150. That was the beginning of a glorious life buying all types of riding horses and ponies, mainly in Ireland, and bringing them over to Melton Mowbray. Here they would be prepared for sale by Barbara and, later, her head groom of thirty-four years, David Bland – the best nagsman in the business – at her immaculate yard. Tell Barbara what you are looking for and she will find it for you.

Horse breeding in Ireland today is very similar to its practice in nineteenth-century England – a profitable form of farm diversification. Barbara used to travel all over Ireland, visiting farmers who might have a likely young horse, but over the last fifteen years she has tended to buy more from wholesale dealers who know the form and know where good horses can be found. They will take an order for a 13.2-hand pony or a 17-hand heavy hunter and come up with the goods. Irish horses have become so expensive that it is now prudent to buy through wholesale dealers against whom there would be some form of redress if a horse turned out to be unsatisfactory. 'The beauty of five-year-old Irish horses,' Barbara told me, 'is that they tend to be honest sorts and you are getting them before they have been abused or spoilt. When you start work on them you are not correcting someone else's faults.'

In an average year Barbara will handle more than fifty horses. The wholesale dealers buy their horses from horse auctions (such as Goresbridge and Cavan), horse fairs (including those at Tallow and Ballinasloe) and other places throughout the country. I asked her whether she ever bought horses abroad. 'Not as a general rule,' she told me. 'I've built my reputation on Irish horses, but there are some wonderful ones in Poland, East Germany and Russia, particularly the Ukraine. Holland too. I've been on buying trips with friends all over Europe but the horse fairs in Holland have to be seen to be believed. In Zuidlaren and Hedel whole streets are roped off, with young horses tethered shoulder to shoulder being trotted up and down for inspection. Absolutely fascinating. You'd love it.'

Given a bit of time I know Barbara could have found the perfect mount for Clarissa but the foot and mouth crisis has seriously affected her business. The hunters she showed us would have made my old dad's eyes gleam, but a 16.2 Irish five-year-old was not quite what we were looking for. In our case I think prudence is the key, at any rate to begin with. A couple of seasons on a nice, sturdy, long-suffering 15.2 cob, about ten years old and absolutely bombproof. Something Clarrie can get on and off easily, should the necessity arise. We need to go somewhere not too energetic: open country without any heart-stopping obstacles that might cause a little tumble. Moorland hunting with the Glaisdale or the Goathland, if they would have us. As it happens, I was in a pub near Danby not long ago and met this bloke who said he'd got just the thing...

CHAPTER FIVE

'The Forgotten Bloodsport'

It has always seemed to me that, of all the field sports, fishing is the one that requires the greatest dedication. When hunting with hounds of whatever variety one is swept along by the energy of the chase, the music of the hounds and the presence of one's fellow followers. There is the competition to keep up with the field and the camaraderie of the waiting periods. You are never alone unless you choose to be or get badly lost. When shooting there is the awareness of your gun and the companionship of the dog, the suspense of the stalk, the noise of the beat, the cries of 'over' and the sighting of the birds. With fishing there is none of that. It is a sport of solitude. Even if you can see someone else on the same beat, they will be as cocooned as you in their world of rod and water.

Fishing requires faith. You look hopefully into the deep pools of the river or the churning surf of the ocean in the belief that there is a fish worthy of your efforts lurking somewhere in the depths, and trust that, by some chemistry of guile, interpretation of its desires and the weather conditions, and a little bit of luck, you will land it.

All this is done in some discomfort. Hot bright weather doesn't yield fish, but hot, muggy, overcast weather of the kind beloved by biting insects is good. Light rain is excellent. Indeed fishermen welcome almost any rain short of a hurricane. If you fish from a small boat, its motion will not be conducive to serenity. If you fish from the shore the insects will have a wonderful picnic, and you can hook anything from various parts of your anatomy to chunks of the scenery. Waders are hot, uncomfortable and dangerous (although I have to confess to finding thigh waders unbearably sexy on a man). If you trip in waders they will fill with water and there is a distinct possibility of drowning.

Despite all this we love it. Whether sitting patiently by a disused gravel pit, casting into a gin-clear stream or throwing a line into the sea, fishing is totally addictive. It is an immensely popular sport: four million fishermen can't be wrong and that's in Britain alone. When we were at Endsleigh on the Tamar in the last series, Horace Adams, the water bailiff of Johnny's boyhood, described how Johnny's grandmother had slipped and fallen into the Tamar while fishing in chest waders and was rescued within an inch of her life. Next day she was back in the Tamar almost up to her chin. I rest my case.

I started with sea fishing when I was about ten years old. I was sent to stay with a small cousin and her parents in Donegal in the far west of Ireland. Remember, I was a sophisticated London child who lived in great comfort surrounded by servants. I found myself in a remote village where the drinking water had to be brought from the pump at the top of the hill in buckets (usually, it seemed, by me), and the milk fetched in a small churn across the fields. I hated it. The place was boring (or rather, I was bored) and hostile. My cousins were Protestant holiday incomers in a totally Catholic village, although the locals relaxed with me when they discovered I was Catholic too. The village shop and shebeen, O'Cohen's, was run by a swarthy man who wore a bowler hat and lacked anything I might conceivably want to buy. To pile Pelion on to Ossa, my cousin's mother was the most dreadful cook, reburning for dinner the overcooked lamb we had had for lunch. However, there were redeeming moments.

The cottage was right by the sea and I made my first solo essay at cooking by dragging large crabs from under rocks at low tide with a bent wire coat hanger and boiling them in a galvanised bucket of seawater over a driftwood fire. They were delicious. This crab hunting was great sport in itself. I went with a local boy a few years older than me called Shaun and was greatly envious of him because he had a much superior tool. This was a long steel hook bound on to a wooden handle with a fierce point on the end. I don't remember that it was any more efficient than my unravelled coat hanger (the sort you get from dry cleaners) but it looked the part. Moreover, Shaun told me with great pride that at the spring equinoctial tides, when the sea receded much further, he and his father went after lobsters with just such hooks.

Our beach had great piles of very black rocks and at low tide we waded through the rock pools, probing with our hooks. The knack was to wiggle the wire gently under the crab with the hook down, then spin it round and hoik the crab out before the beast had time to jam itself into the crevice. Speed and dexterity were needed and it was great fun. If the crab won the first bout, you marked the hole and moved on until it settled down. Shaun said the local fishermen used to tie a dead fish to one end of a piece of twine and a rag to the other, and the crab would take the bait back to his hole and mark it. I never saw this done but we agreed it was more fun not knowing whether a hole was occupied before we started our probing.

I was slightly in awe of the crabs, which were a good size (or so they seemed to me) with large claws which could give a nasty nip. The way to carry them was to wait until you had two, then put them together in a fierce embrace and hold them by the hind legs. I suspect Shaun was showing off, as we had a perfectly good bucket. My first piece of practical culinary knowledge was that you shouldn't put crabs into boiling water because they shoot their main claws which lets the water into the body and makes them rather wet eating. You never try and eat the deadmen's fingers more than once but contrary to belief they aren't poisonous.

One day my cousin announced that Mark was coming with the boat and we were going after the fish. In Ireland one is always assumed to know who everyone is and it is always 'the' boat or 'the' fish, never 'a'. As I soon discovered, we were going mackerel fishing in a large cobbler. This is a wooden clinker-built boat with a pointed bow and a rounded stern, much used in coastal waters. The boat has very little in the way of keel and is landed stern first, the sharp prow keeping off the waves. The motion in choppy seas is legendary. Mackerel fishing is a perfect introduction for young children. I was given a hand line with a great many large hooks on it and a bag of dyed red feathers and told to attach them to the hooks, which I succeeded in doing with no major injury. These large hooks are used when the mackerel are running in shoals as they can be quickly removed from the fish's mouth. When we reached the right spot the lines were put over the side and Mark took up the oars again. Almost at once I felt tugs on the line and pulled it in under Mark's instruction.

Attached to the hooks were a great many fish. Shoaling mackerel are rather stupid. When they are running they will bite at almost anything bright in the water (tin foil is excellent), and will practically leap into the boat. The lightest of weights is used when the fish are so near the surface; a one-ounce weight will do nicely. If they are being timid, shiny dried fish skin is a good bait, and I'm told a twist of tobacco also works well. Best of all, reputedly, is a strip of mackerel skin cut from the tail and attached to a piece of cork. All of these are necessary when the fish are shy or at some depth, but for a spring run anything will do.

A freshly caught mackerel is a thing of beauty, iridescent with silver and other gleaming colours and exuding muscular vitality. I am not by nature squeamish so I banged them on the head quite happily and after a period of high excitement and activity we rowed back to shore with nearly a hundred fish. Mackerel fresh from the sea cooked over a fire on the beach are

Fishing boats in Ireland

heaven, but for every hour thereafter the taste degenerates. I can never buy the lacklustre fish one sees even in the best fishmonger's and only eat it if it has just been caught. Mark took most of the fish as, in a rural community in the 1950s, they were an important food source, and we were left with about twenty-five. After we had eaten our fill we decided to stop passing cars and sell the rest. We wrapped the fish in newspaper, got sixpence for each of them and were delighted with our efforts.

Mackerel have always been a vital economic crop to poor communitities. In 1895, a dark time in Irish history, 467,560 barrels were landed off the west and southern Irish coasts at a value of £152,512. Of these, 51,000 barrels were cured and sent to America, mostly to New York, which had an insatiable appetite for pickled mackerel. On talking to a Swedish friend I discovered that this is also a great Swedish delicacy but one I have never come across elsewhere. When the mackerel shoals failed in America in the 1890s, boats sought the fish as far away as Norway and the west coast of Africa.

Mackerel shoals stand far out to sea in winter and come inshore in the late spring. Their arrival is viewed as a harbinger of summer. Stories of mackerel fishing abound. Elian, a great storyteller, tells that mackerel were trained as decoys to lead shoals into the fishermen's nets. A Norwegian story tells of a bather being surrounded by a shoal and nibbled and driven out to sea, where he was rescued by the arrival of a fishing boat but died of loss of blood from his wounds. A possibly inebriated Admiral Pleyville-Lepley recounted how off the Greenland coast, where the water is clear, thousands of mackerel are to be seen with their heads stuck in the mud and their tails in the air as a means of overwintering, a tale which bears a distinct resemblance to the old country belief that swallows, with which mackerel are often compared, wintered in the mud at the bottom of ponds.

All these stories Mark told me (the Irish are great raconteurs) on the occasions I went out with him again. The other children fell by the wayside but I found mackerel fishing totally consuming. I have since learnt that Donegal Bay, especially the coast round Rossbeg, is a prime mackerel area and so it was a happy introduction to fishing. I have fished for mackerel since, mostly off the beach or in the evening, when they will come into small harbours and move among the boats. I have caught the great king mackerel off yachts in the West Indies and very good eating they were too, but the most magic memories remain in Donegal Bay.

Leaving Donegal, I went south to the Dingle peninsula to stay with my father's anaesthetist Lawrence Morris, his wife Mary and their teenage son Richard. This was a great contrast as they were happy, plump, food-loving people and were incredibly sweet to me, as I now see. Lawrence and Richard were enjoying a father and son fishing holiday and the presence of a small girl can hardly have been their idea of a popular addition. They took me salmon fishing, which I didn't enjoy. We tramped miles through peat hags riven with midges to reach a river. There they equipped me with a rod and left me to my own devices. I caught a small par and was reduced to tears when required to put it back. It all seemed such an effort after my bounteous mackerel!

I enjoyed the fishing for sea bass off the coast rather more. The strange silver light of that part of Ireland at evening was very magical. The fish were running but I did not catch one. However, I did succeed in hooking what I remain convinced was a Dover sole. It was more probably a flounder of some sort and I hooked it through the eye socket. I remember being immensely proud and bearing it back to be cooked by 'Auntie' Mary for my supper. I was a lonely and unhappy child until I went to boarding school and met my friend Christine and the other dear Colemans and so acquired a 'proper family', and this holiday of sea fishing gave me an affection for the sport which has remained with me ever since.

The best sporting sea fish is probably the bass, which the Irish will persist in calling a king mullet. The sea bass is actually a large marine perch. It has a dark blue back, silvery sides and belly, and plenty of teeth, some in a crescent at the roof of the mouth and others in a patch at the base of the tongue. Its mouth is leathery and tough. It has a row of sharp spines along its back which arch angrily when it is caught and on which you can prick yourself quite nastily.

Bass are to be found at sea in spring and summer, coming into the estuaries to breed in the autumn. Shoal bass are usually younger, smaller fish, averaging between two and five pounds. If you are fishing a shoal from a boat, the boat can't be taken into the shoal as with mackerel but must hover at the edge of the channel where the fish are feeding while the angler casts across them. If you draw the fish you have caught downstream, you will not alarm the other fish, which will be feeding facing towards the current. Shoals feed on whitebait or sand eels and you can usually spot them by the presence of gulls and the splashing of hunting fish. We found a man in Devon who used to be sent to the clifftop as a young man to watch for the shoals of bass feeding: his eyesight was so fine that he could distinguish the colours of the bass from any other feeding shoal. The best time to catch them is about an hour after the turn of the tide in overcast weather.

The biggest bass live singly or in groups of three or four. You can sometimes see them cruising round small harbours or off a pier in a bay, but they are very disdainful and hard to catch in these conditions. The best chance you have of catching a really big mature loner is off rocks at the evening rise with the tide coming in. This brings the small fish in close to the shore to feed with the bass following. It is the most dramatic fishing, with the surf churning silver and red in the rays of the setting sun and the whole sea reflecting back the low light. The soughing of the sea and the crying of the odd gull gives the whole a mystic air and one feels unseen companions who have fished off the self-same rocks in days long gone.

My friend Christine is married to a mad keen bass fisherman, Douglas, and I used to go camping with them on the coast in Brittany. In the evening Douglas would go off to fish the 'fiendly rokkes black' of Chaucer's 'The Knight's Tale'. He used an interesting local technique, known as a *boule d'eau* or bowl of water. This is a plastic ball you fill with water to provide the weight. It is transparent and scentless and, with an artificial sand eel, proved very successful. One of the great advantages of the *boule d'eau* is that you don't have to cart heavy weights around. All you carry is a nice light object which you then fill up with water – an omnipresent feature of fishing – and hey presto! you have your weight. He fished in the gaps between the rocks and usually brought back a couple of good bass for supper. There is nothing better than sitting by the barbecue on a fine French evening eating a freshly caught, simply grilled bass with Hollandaise made by me with a fork and irascible elbow grease.

Such fishing is of course made much easier by modern tackle, with light carbon rods, modern easy-to-use reels and nylon line, but it was not always thus. I borrowed one of Johnny's books from the Badminton Library series, written at the end of the nineteenth century. Johnny has a fine collection of such books, either bought by him or inherited from his father Walter. At times when nothing is in season or the weather is too foul, he mopes over

East coast throw out

them, his marmalade curls reflecting in the reading lamp as he yearns for the days when all sport was very uncomfortable and insanely brave. 'I say, Clarrie,' he cries, 'this is the thing: fishing for giant sturgeon with hooks under the ice on the Sea of Azoff. You bore holes through the ice and let down lines three foot long and a foot apart and you might catch a fish of two thousand seven hundred pounds. Wonder if they still do it, how would we get there?' 'Rather chilly,' I venture. With the look of scorn I have known so well ever since, aged eleven, I was foolish enough to complain tearfully that, in getting the hook out of the perch we had caught on the Piskers' pond, he had driven it into my thumb, he rounds on me. 'Don't be so wet. You'd look very jolly in sables, and besides, we could take a thermos and you know you love caviar,' and he dashes off to get an atlas. Still, enough of that. Incidentally, the Sea of Azoff is north of Finland.

In the Badminton Library book there is an account of suitable tackle for fishing bass from the shore. The book is dated 1895 and there is a wonderful picture of a man hurling the end of a handline, to which is attached a lead weight, into the sea, rather in the manner of a cricketer fielding on the boundary throwing in a long ball. This is referred to as an 'East Coast Throw-Out Line' and the writer, one John Bickerdyke, describes it thus:

> At the end of the line proper is a piece of finer line, eight feet in length and about as thick as common whipcord. The lead weighs about a pound, and is fixed to the whipcord... by

> means of a strip of leather put through the hole in the lead. At the other end of the whipcord is a button. The hooks begin at the end of the main line, and may number from six to twenty or even more; they are fixed on snoods seven inches long and placed fourteen inches apart. A necessary part of the tackle is a broom handle six feet long with a cleft cut at the end of it, and the whole line when not in use is wound on a winder... The two side pieces of the winder are eighteen inches in length, and they are placed eight inches apart. This tackle is used in the following way. The line is uncoiled and spread out in S-shaped curves on the beach, the landward end of it being fastened firmly to the winder, which is stuck into the sand. The hooks are then baited, and... the button on the end of the whipcord is placed in the cleft of the stick. The exact position of the lead on the whipcord must depend on the height of the caster and the length of the pole, a short man having to slip it up rather nearer the button than a tall man.
>
> By means of the pole the lead is now swung backwards and then pitched forwards, not too straight, but rather up in the air, for the weight and the line has to be raised. It is not always necessary to cast out a great distance, for sometimes fish will be feeding close along shore.

Just as well.

I never cease to be amazed at the ingenuity of man in search of sport or food and I suspect the picture of the man hand hurling which is next to the picture of the superior man with the broomstick is what happens after repeated broomstick failure. I have high hopes for Johnny fishing with this tackle. He was good at cricket and always fielded on the boundary for Ripe and Chalvington. This was not only for his strong right arm but so that he could chat up the birds and have a quick Pimm's, but I'm sure all the techniques remain.

Bass fishermen are as pernickety as fly fishermen about the best bait to use. Douglas will wax eloquent on the use of squid or skate liver as yielding marvellous results. Small mussels are apparently also good for bait. All these are used for tempting the large loners. It is interesting that in so many forms of sport it is the older creature, outside the herd or shoal and at the end of its breeding prime, that is the most sought after as a trophy beast, all its cunning and knowledge pitted against the sportsman. I should like to go thus rather than in age and infirmity.

Since bass tend to eat small fry or sand eels as a general rule, these are also good tempting bait and many happy hours can be spent acquiring them. Bait digging or fishing is the light comedy of real fishing. The humble lugworm is spurned as unsporting but, as I always say, it depends how hungry you are – and if you are fishing off the East Anglian coast the bass will take little else. There is a picture of Douglas as a grinning small boy holding up a three-pound bass which he and his father caught on a lugworm off Cromer pier. Lugworms are the natural bait on the East Anglian coast as sand eel is not common there, which may explain why the locals have no problems but the rest of the world thinks that that is not a bass coast. Good bass have been caught off the old Martello towers around that coast. A bass is a fine fighting fish and far and away the best eating, but one must not underestimate the sporting abilities of both the pollack and the grey mullet. However, as all my culinary skills have never succeeded in making the latter anything more than tolerable, I shall move swiftly on.

Bass can be caught on a fly, especially in the autumn, when they come into the estuaries. They will take a fly when feeding on herring fry and are close to the surface. Flyfishing is only effective on school bass. The best fly for bass is a 'whitebait' fly made originally from the dried shredded tail of a dogfish. A bass will also take a fly under the water, so it is necessary to watch the line if your fly sinks. If the bass are fishing on sand eels, artificial ones can be used. These are nowadays bought in tackle shops but Mr Bickerdyke recommends making one with a length of copper bell wire and a length of greyish-white rubber as used for feeding bottles (and heaven knows what else), the back coloured with Stephen's blue-black ink and the belly covered in silver foil with two pink India rubber beads to represent eyes. One can imagine the havoc the author must have caused in his Victorian household, disconnecting bell pulls, snatching the bottle from the baby and even cutting up Mrs Bickerdyke's corset (for whence else could come the pink India rubber?).

Johnny and I went fishing in Tor Bay with Len, the nephew of the keen-eyed bass spotter. We went out in a fairly large boat so that we had to fish off the shoal bank rather than under the cliffs, but we had a lovely time. Using sand eels as bait, Len caught six good fish, Johnny three and two mackerel, and I caught two (but I bet they were the biggest!). I had to throw two others back as they were undersized: by law, you cannot land any bass under 17 inches in length. The small bass that you see in the shops are farmed. Bass are heavily farmed now, some off the UK coast but largely off Greece and Turkey. They are not bad as farmed fish, though a little flabby, and are best barbecued as this firms them up and gives them a good taste.

A fish you don't see much nowadays is the conger eel, which brings us to a lively tale. We came to glatting by an outside straight. You may remember Johnny's passion for terriers, exampled by the fact that his childhood photo album had twenty-five pictures of terriers and twenty-five of ferrets and naught else! This passion is not shared by all of us to the same extreme, which fault Johnny decided to remedy by any means. One day when the people from the BBC happened to be around, he embarked on his account of glatting: 'This was a practice in times past which was used for fishing for conger eels in the Bristol Channel. Usually these monsters of the deep move with the tide but in the Bristol Channel the tide goes out so far that the congers, who are notoriously lazy, retire under rocks where they wait bad-temperedly for

'Mine's definitely bigger than yours'

the return of the sea. The locals would go out with a mixed pack of dogs, which would sniff out the congers and set up a cry. The fisherman would then prise up and overturn the stone and the furious conger would set off, lickety-split, towards the distant sea, pursued by dogs and fishermen alike until the fisherman overtook it and pinioned it with a trident spear.'

Like all great raconteurs, Johnny loves to play the emotions of his listeners like a harp and the BBC team became very excited about the idea of filming this. Johnny was hoist with the petard of his own success as he had to bring them back down to reality. After a lifetime of rising to such baits and soaring to heights of enthusiasm only to find Johnny grinning sardonically, I watched the whole with great joy. However, glatting does exist, although in a very limited way, so off we set to the Bristol Channel to look under rocks for conger eels. We took Tug for colour – not quite as good as a mixed pack, but a conger is a nasty beast which moves at speed.

Conger is excellent in pies, where it adds a splendid texture. It is also great in fish soup. It

'Rubbish'

has a very delicate flavour and is delicious roasted in cider with an apple at each end. It is also popular in West Indian cooking. There was a time when dried conger was the single largest export from Cornwall to France and it was a valuable commercial fish.

Fishing for conger can be great fun if you are prepared for it. Congers prefer soft bait, and a cuttlefish heavily beaten like a tough steak is very successful, as is a chunk of stale sourdough bread flavoured with fish paste. One of the worst problems is the conger's formidable teeth and in order to prevent them breaking the line a snood should be used. You can of course use chain as if for pike but the set of the conger's teeth is such that if you cover the line with a hemp snood it will embed its teeth into the hemp (which should be wound round with copper wire to secure it) and hang on for dear life. Fishing for congers over rocks is not to be recommended as the fish will wedge itself under a rock and even the strongest of pulls is unlikely to detach it. If one is fishing at night or late evening over a sandy bottom one may catch very large congers, or 'serpents', as the Scots call them. Landing these at night in a small boat is a frightening experience but they fight as well as any game fish and are good sport. Like all eels the conger has a pernicious habit of twisting round and round in the water and trying to climb up the line as you try to land it, so remember to fit a swivel of some desciption if you are fishing for them or they will break the line.

Let me tell you about my unpleasant experience with a conger eel. My mother, my brother and a small me were fishing off Arran for codling. Nowadays if you want to fish for cod inshore or off rocks you need to go to Newfoundland, because the Common Fisheries Policy of the EU has allowed the Spaniards et al to fish them to extinction around our coasts. I met a woman recently who described how she had been fishing in a small boat off Newfoundland whilst the sea eagles swooped down to take the codling off her hook. In my youth, however, they were good local fishing. Douglas regularly caught them on worm off the beach in Norfolk. On the occasion in question my brother hooked a good fish and was about to land it when a conger eel locked on to the codling and embedded its teeth well into the fish. My brother was loath to go home empty-handed (we were into the gloaming by then) and succeeded in landing the whole shebang with the help of a large gaff. There we sat in our small boat with a seven-pound conger, a half-dead codling and a small priest. The conger resisted all efforts to dispatch it using the priest and thrashed about alarmingly. It let go of the cod and snapped about with its fearsome teeth. In the end my brother cut its head off and quite ruined his fishing knife.

The coarse side of fishing is huge business, with many millions of enthusiasts, and of course the deep-sea side of it attracts huge international interest. Coarse fishermen tend to think their sport is not at risk from the antis but Pisces, a campaign for the abolition of angling, describe fishing as a bloodsport and have made it quite clear that they seek to ban fishing of all kinds. Saboteurs rely on Pisces for information about disrupting coarse fishing contests. Some of them then turn up to interrupt these contests using the sort of tactics used against hunts. According to Pisces, the RSPCA is against angling. When I rang the RSPCA they told me that, although they have no plans to campaign against fishing at present, they are concerned for 'the feelings of the fish' and may become more active in the future.

I want to preserve my right to fish. I live by a river that was formerly a fair salmon river. It even has a Victorian salmon ladder. The building of a paper factory polluted the river and killed off most of the fish, but today the factory is defunct and the river cleaned up. There are plenty of brown trout and we look eagerly for salmon to return. However, the water bailiffs are hampered by legislation protecting the shags, the seals and even the herons. There is a huge heronry and while I love to see them it is all a question of balance. Personally I take home and eat any good-sized brown trout I catch, which, given my skill levels, isn't many. What could be nicer than to rise early, catch the dawn and breakfast well? Dream on, Clarissa.

'To hunt the glatt'

Johnny was slightly glum on the day we set off glatting. Tug had not excelled at the terrier racing, and even the rosette in the working terrier class had not lifted his spirits. As we set off to meet Somerset's last glatter, Cliff Beaver, Tug was in fine fettle, bouncing around in the car, barking at passing dogs and revelling in the quality time he was spending snuggled up on Johnny's knee. Terriers tend to be one-person dogs and while Tug is the most gregarious of souls and will bestow his favours on most of the human race, he is Johnny's dog, heart and soul, and I suspect it is a two-way transaction.

We arrived at Blue Anchor beach to be welcomed warmly by Cliff. He is clearly an old-fashioned countryman with joy in all the old sports and foods, and he proudly presented me with a jar of lava (this, to the uninitiated, is a type of seaweed which is eaten in Wales fried for breakfast with bacon and cockles). It is delicious, but his wife gets tired of his offerings. The beach is a long rocky cove surrounded by high headlands ribbed with seams of alabaster. The rock strata on the beach break down in infinitesimal steps which makes walking very difficult. Johnny, whose perfectionism puts me to shame with monotonous regularity, demanded to know what this rock formation is called. I don't know and not being a geologist I don't really care, so I said it was *oliticus uncomfortabilis*, at which he snorted and stomped off.

Cliff had brought his spaniel, which he uses to sniff out and mark the congers, and the dogs frolicked together on the beach quite happily. We tramped along, talking about Cliff's poles. He has one straight green plastic one which is fairly rigid and one hazel twig as straight as possible, cut from a coppice. The disadvantage of the hazel stick is that it only lasts three or four trips before breaking, and if the bark peels off into the hole, the conger will not return to it. Glatt is the West Country name for a conger eel, and apparently comes from a Norse word for a sea monster. One hears fearsome tales of hundred-pound beasts with heads the size of a dog's and a ten-inch girth. Cliff once caught a twenty-five-pound glatt but says the trawlers have destroyed the trade. When he was younger he could go out on the beach and catch any number of good-sized fish but now they tend to be around the ten-pound mark.

We set off across the beach in pursuit of the fast receding tide, me hanging on behind the cameraman on the quad bike and clutching equipment. Suddenly the dogs got very excited and rushed to a fissure in the rock. We peered into the hole and saw the end of a conger's tail in a hole about six inches across. The spaniel ran around wagging his tail and barking, and Tug went into that still, pointing mode that signals he is focusing on a kill. Remember, Tug has never seen a conger and his only trip to the beach was when he was a puppy. I asked Cliff how he intended getting the fish out, as it was head into the runnel and couldn't turn. He hoped the runnel had another exit and was poking about in a pool when Tug struck. Fortunately the camera was following him, so with any luck the nation will see it, for it was a most amazing performance. He grabbed the tail as far above its end as he could and hauled out a conger about four feet long. Then he splatted it on a rock, grabbed it behind the head and shook it like a rat. When Cliff went to kill it, it was already stone dead. Later Tug caught another slightly bigger fish and, having killed that too, proceeded to eat its head to see what it tasted like. I must admit I spent a lot of the subsequent car journey waiting to see if he had digested it, but fortunately there were no ill effects.

One now understands how they glatted with terriers, but what was amazing was Tug's natural behaviour. The antis who protest that it is man who urges on the dog were quite confounded. Tug was on to the eels and he had no knowledge or training to hunt them. It was pure and simple instinct.

We suddenly noticed that the tide was coming in fast, so I had an even more hair-raising journey back on the quad across very uneven rocks and quaggy mud to beat the tide. This boded well for the horse, I felt, as I stayed on and wasn't stiff the next day. I barbecued conger collops on a beach fire and all agreed they were very good. Johnny was cock-a-hoop as we piled into my Saab, his spirits quite uplifted by Tug's success. One very muddy, rather smelly little dog was much applauded by both of us and fell happily asleep on Johnny's knee to dream of glatts.

JAMES PURDEY & SONS,
LTD.
GUN & RIFLE MAKERS
AUDLEY HOUSE,
SOUTH AUDLEY STREET,
LONDON, W.1

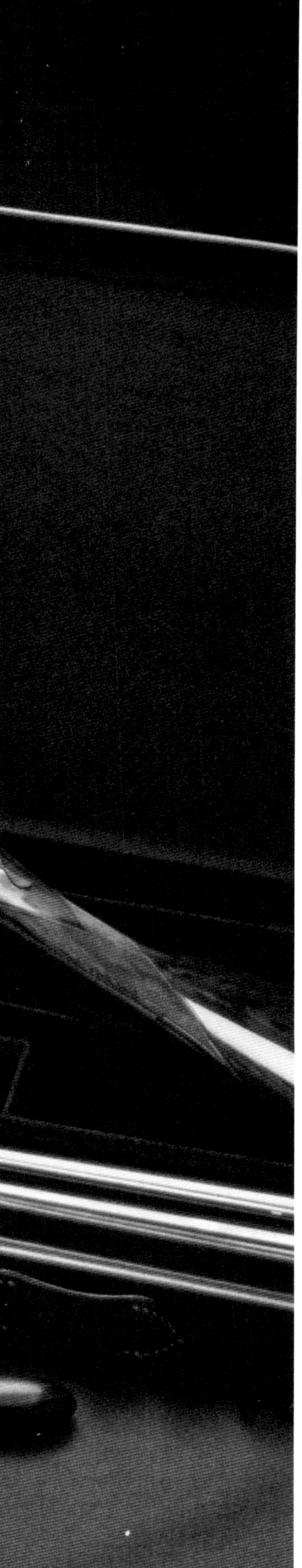

CHAPTER SIX

'NEVER, NEVER LET YOUR ...

My tenth birthday present was a rook rifle made by Holland & Holland before the First World War and bored out in the1920s to take a .410 cartridge. I was, as may be imagined, thrilled to bits. I had longed for something to shoot with but airguns had been forbidden on the grounds that they would spoil my eye. I was less thrilled to discover that it would be some time before a live cartridge was placed in the breech and I was allowed to practise on clays. First I needed to learn the essentials of gun safety and all the verses of 'A Father's Advice to his Son' ('Never, never let your gun/Pointed be at anyone').

This is the age when children can best be taught not only the lore of the countryside, the habitat and seasons for game, but also the manners, courtesies and behaviour of the shooting field. They are dead keen and therefore receptive. Much of what I know I learnt on walks beside my father, carrying my unloaded .410. More I learnt from old Joe Botting, our pigman, who took me ferreting, or Frank Chilman, the man from whom my father used to buy terriers, by then working as a keeper on the Brookhouse estate. Some I discovered with Tiger, the terrier I had at that age, as we stealthily crept along hedgerows together in the hope of a shot at a pheasant, or stalked expectantly up to ponds and the occasional unsuspecting mallard.

When I was thirteen, I graduated to a 16 bore made by Cogswell & Harrison – 'a Birmingham gun', my father said dismissively – that had been shot and regulated by Hollands. My father shot with a 12 bore and would never allow a smaller 20 bore (which some might consider the natural progression from a .410) in the house for fear of a 20-bore cartridge getting in among the 12s and slipping unnoticed past the chambers. As a JP he had been shown the police photographs of the remains of someone who had made that mistake. I shot with this little gun for the next eight years and would go up to the Holland & Holland shooting school at the start of every season for an afternoon with Mr Gage, their instructor. My father shot with a Holland Royal, a beautiful side lock ejector with detachable locks, distinctive acanthus scroll engraving and a French walnut stock, its dark veins sweeping forward from the heel to the action. It was one of a pair made for my great-grandfather in 1898. My grandfather had the other gun and, together with their leather travelling cases, snap caps and ebony-handled turnscrews and cleaning rods, they were a magnificent example of the best English guns, the epitome of balance, grace and efficiency. When I was twenty-one my grandfather gave me his gun and there was another trip to Holland & Holland to have it fitted to me.

During my late teens and twenties I shot a lot – as much as hunting would allow – and am very lucky and privileged to have done so. I remember with particular happiness the annual trip to the Isle of Wight where my father's great friend Robert Clarke had a shoot near Carisbrooke Castle. Standing at our pegs, we waited patiently for the spectacular high birds, glinting against the sunlight as they came in over the downs behind Mottistone. I remember with equal pleasure shooting on the Cooling Marshes that run up to the Thames Estuary on the Isle of Grain. Lying up in the reeds beside the big fleet that ran alongside the sea wall, waiting for the pinkfeet to start flighting inland as dawn broke, then tramping for miles after the cunning marsh pheasants and the coveys of partridges. In the late afternoon we lay up again as widgeon and teal came flitting through the gloaming. All this and glorious birdsong only twelve miles from the centre of London.

There was a period when I almost stopped shooting. Lloyd's had swallowed up the Hollands and I was farming seven days a week simply to keep afloat. A couple of days through the season was all I could manage. When Sam was seven, an old friend, Tommy, who came out rabbiting most weekends through the winter, unexpectedly gave him a little .410. It was a poacher's gun that folded so you could conceal it inside your coat. Tommy is a typical example of the urban countryman. In those days he ran a stall at East Fortune open market on Sundays and other places like Berwick-on-Tweed during the week. He picks up through the grouse season with his cocker spaniel and beats on the low-ground pheasant shoots through

Carisbrooke Castle

the winter. Like most of the beaters and picker-uppers in this part of the world, he lives on one of the peripheral estates round Edinburgh, but the same will be true throughout the country. Huge numbers of agricultural workers have gone off the land since 1950, and beating or picking up on the weekends gives some of them a chance to get back into the country. Many landlords are only too happy for those that help in the season to come out and do a bit of pest control such as rabbiting and pigeoning during the rest of the year. There is an incalculable added advantage to rural communities in this since, with the police force being chronically undermanned, we have had to set up countryside crime watch schemes. People like Tommy know what goes on in their own patches, which are often the same areas from which a lot of our trouble emanates. They are fiercely protective of their rural roots and act as our eyes and ears. Many an urban poacher has had a visit from an unexpected source and a little chat that proves more salutary than police intervention.

I had not intended to start 'passing it on' to Sam until he was about ten but Tommy's kind present coincided with an advertisement in the *Shooting Times* for a British Association for

Shooting and Conservation (BASC) Young Guns day being run locally. BASC and the Countryside Alliance organise innumerable such days annually to introduce the young to field sports, which are vital to the continuity of the countryside. These events are especially useful for people who are thinking of a career in wildlife management but do not live in the country or have easy access to its activities.

Field sports are under a two-pronged attack: one the threat of a Government ban, the other one of attrition. Gun licences are becoming more and more difficult to obtain by legitimate sportsmen, although this legislation makes no impact on the illegal possession of firearms. There is now talk of no one under the age of eighteen being allowed to use a shotgun. The Campaign for Shooting and the BASC are fiercely resisting this, not only because it infringes on personal liberties but more so because denying the young the opportunity to learn gun safety at an early age – something they will never fully acquire later – also denies them the opportunity to learn about the countryside.

You can never teach a child gun safety too early. The only limitation is the recoil of a shotgun. I am glad Sam started at seven, since it gave us three more years together exploring our priceless heritage and a shared passion. We had ferreted together using nets for several years and in due course we started bolting the rabbits to the gun. Bolting bunnies is terrific fun, and wonderful discipline for a boy. Clarrie often came with us, sitting on her stool as a gleeful spectator, revelling in Sam's successes and sometimes having a go with his .410. At one time she owned a pair of 20 bores and she would reminisce wistfully about the period in her life when she ran a pheasant farm and had an old French hammer gun that she used about the place. Knowing that Clarrie was prowling around the woodland adjoining the rearing pens, armed to the teeth, must have been as reassuring to the pheasant poults as it would have been alarming to any predator who ran into her.

In March, the editor of the *Shooting Times*, Julian Murray-Evans, had asked us to the annual Woodcock Dinner for people who have achieved that most difficult shot, a right and left, at these delicious birds. On this occasion it was held in the great hall of Durham Castle. On the way into dinner we passed a long refectory table on which the items for auction were displayed. I discovered Clarissa, who had gone on ahead of me, lovingly handling a hammer gun donated by D. J. Litt of Newport, the largest gun retailers in the country. It was a very pretty little 16 bore with a Jones rotary underlever, back action locks and an attractive dark-grained stock, made by G. E. Lewis of Birmingham, as famous as any of the Midland gunmakers in his day. 'When do you think it was made?' Clarrie asked, her face wreathed in smiles.

The history of old guns is absolutely fascinating because there were so many gunmakers. Leaving aside the Birmingham and London trade, there were over two hundred provincial gunmakers in 1900. Because of the speed at which gunmaking technology progressed after 1860, there was a relatively short period during which good hammer guns were made, and most became victims of abuse and neglect. Those that survive retain much of the grace and elegance of a flintlock. This one still had some of the original case hardening round the action. The barrels were steel rather than Damascus, which put it towards the end of the century. 'Perhaps 1885,' I hazarded.

'Price?' I was quite surprised she bothered to ask. Clarrie had that look about her which indicates that she wants something and is determined to have it. The eyes protrude slightly, the head goes down, the shoulders come up. The torso bends at the stomach, hands clench into fists. There are those about who know what I mean.

'Well,' I said, 'the Americans are grabbing every decent hammer gun they can find. I reckon you could sell it to the States for about three thousand. You might be lucky here but gaw canny over fifteen hundred.'

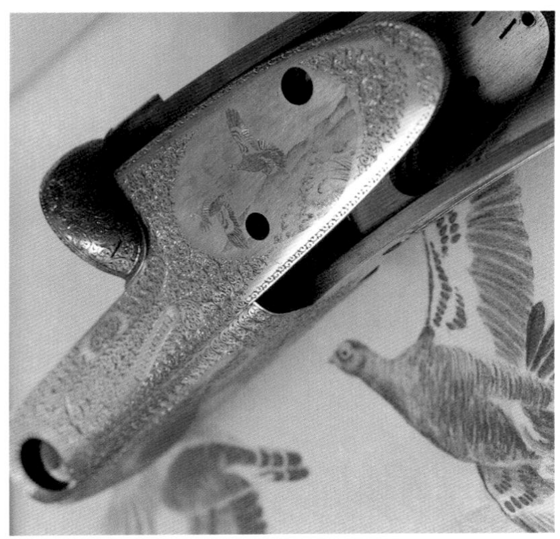

An engraving of partridges in flight

'Hmmf,' she said.

The outcome was never in any doubt and I have rarely seen her as chuffed. 'My own gun,' she prattled happily on our way back to stay with Peter and Sheila Lister. 'My own gun.'

D. J. Litt were offering not only to fit the gun but also to have it engraved. As it happened, the gun had previously belonged to Simon Gudgeon, the famous wildlife artist, and he kindly agreed to draw a woodcock which could then be copied by an engraver. As soon as possible after the Woodcock Dinner we set forth for Newport on a little outing which would also include popping in to see Allan Myers, a gunmaker friend of mine in Lancashire.

Allan Myers' speciality, apart from his normal gun repair business, is refurbishing and selling big-bore shotguns. He also, periodically, makes them from scratch and is currently making a single- barrel 1 bore. This is the sort of gun that Colonel Peter Hawker, the father of wildfowling, would have salivated over and is probably the first shoulder gun of its size to have been made in over a hundred years. His workshop is a treasure house of high-technology precision machinery for making the delicate internal parts of gun locks and lathes for barrelmaking. There are racks of wonderful old goose guns, double 10 and 8 bores, single and double 4 bores. Most were made before the end of the nineteenth century and have beautifully

Shotgun cartridges, from 4 bore to .410

patterned Damascus barrels, great meaty hammers and metal heel plates. The makers' names are a roll call of the great gunmakers: Tolley, Reilly, Lewis, Greener, Cogswell, Purdey and Holland. I can never look at these massively heavy, finely balanced guns without hearing that adrenalin-pumping sound of a great multitude of geese stirring on their shore roosts and the rattle of frosty reeds as the dawn breaks on a bitter winter's morning.

I love wildfowling more than any other form of shooting. There are those who simply cannot understand that a successful shot is really rather incidental. The pleasure comes from the sights and sounds of the marshes, the planning that goes into assessing flight patterns, the knowledge of the tides, moon and weather, as well as the cold and the risk of being marooned by fog and a freak tide. Having got it right against all probability, there is that one shot with the same guns the wildfowlers used when they struggled to earn their living supplying the growing towns and cities in the nineteenth century. A modern 12-bore cartridge would probably have nearly the same range but doesn't begin to compare with hauling back the hammers and lifting one of these lovely old guns, feeling the balance counteract the weight and hearing the long lazy boomf of a black powder cartridge detonating.

My son Sam and I spent a memorable day with Allan between Christmas and New Year, flighting geese inland over decoys up in Perthshire. Sam had got the wildfowling bug in a big way and the excuse for dropping in to see Allan now was the off-chance of buying a big-bore goose gun that Sam and I could share. Fathers use these little ploys to get what they want themselves. I remember my father giving me a magnificent leatherbound stalker's spyglass one Christmas when I was fourteen, which I clearly wasn't likely to use until I was substantially older. Old fowling pieces, like good hammer guns, are much in demand now in America and their price has rocketed.

We left empty-handed, but with a promise from Allan to let me know the minute something affordable came in, and set off to Newport and D. J. Litt's emporium in the Maesglas retail estate. Litt's are the country's largest gun retailers, selling in excess of ten thousand guns a year, as opposed to the ninety or a hundred sold by Purdey or Hollands. Litt's shop is a perfect example of the sheer scale of the interest and enthusiasm in modern-day shooting, particularly among those who look forward to a bit of rough shooting and pigeon flighting on winter weekends and clay pigeon shooting through the summer. Everything for the modern gun is on offer here, including a huge choice of shooting clothes and other kit, and there is an incredible variety of reasonably priced modern shotguns, covering the whole range of interest in the sport. Some are specific trap guns with the raised rib, but most are dual-purpose over and unders from more than a dozen continental manufacturers. There are also copies of the best English side by sides from AYA, the Spanish gunmakers, and a big selection of secondhand Birmingham guns as well as rifles and the latest in airguns.

Carl Eriksson, one of their directors, took us into what he called his office, a modern-day equivalent of Purdey's famous longroom, where the finest English side locks are kept with their oak and leather travelling cases. There were Purdeys, Hollands, Beesleys, Hellises, paired guns and singles. Here, Clarissa's little 16 bore had been waiting for her since the Woodcock Dinner, and once the drooling was over, we set off to the Treetops Shooting School at Cefn Logel where Carl had arranged for Graham Cartwright, the chief instructor, to chuck up some clays and see what alterations were needed to make the gun fit her. This makes so much difference. Of recent years, Clarrie has caused a rabbit to change gear using Sam's gun, which was too long in the stock for her, and a snipe to alter course in Northern Ireland. 'Everyone said they thought I'd hit it,' she complained. To be fair, the shot was with a borrowed gun, from a boat and, as Clarrie declared, 'There was a howling gale, the waters of the lough were whipped to a froth and if I hadn't helped the boatman bale, we would probably have sunk. Then you'd have been sorry. Nice people said they thought I'd hit it. If the wretched thing had come down, you'd have been green with envy.' Once her little 16 has been altered, there won't be any need for excuses.

Treetops is D. J. Litt's shooting school in Wales and one of the best laid out grounds I have seen. There are over forty different stands dotted along the sides of a narrow wooded glen, offering clay disciplines for every conceivable game bird: high pheasants, woodcock, teal, driven grouse and partridges, as well as pigeons. For the bouncing bunny there is a clay trap which simulates a rabbit bolting between burrows. Graham took Clarissa into a beginner's stand and ran through gun safety with her. Instructors always take this precaution with a new client, regardless of how much experience they have had. Once this was over, I stuffed a couple of squidgy sponge earplugs in my ears and settled down in a corner of the stand.

Shooting instructors can see shot in the air and as the clays came over Graham would say, 'You're missing below and to the left' or 'Well behind, get the end of your barrels on the clay, follow through and when you can no longer see it, pull the trigger.' Before long Clarrie was hitting them. The little gun fitted her quite well and at the end of the lesson Graham felt that only a small alteration to the heel of the stock was needed. 'How's that flight pond of yours coming along?' she asked me on the way back to the Land Rover. 'Can't wait for September.'

The growth in shooting schools in itself shows the increased popularity in shooting. At Treetops, what with individual tuition, corporate days and competitions, about six thousand people use the grounds annually, firing off about 150,000 cartridges. There are more than thirty major shooting schools and at least a hundred smaller ones. Something in the region of a million people hold firearm certificates in the UK and every year millions upon millions of cartridges are fired, about half of them at shooting schools and clay pigeon shoots.

Competition shooting, initially of live pigeons, started in 1790. Hawker, author of the famous book on wildfowling – *Instructions to Young Sportsmen in all that relates to Guns and shooting* (1814) – was very disapproving, describing it as 'a glorious opportunity for assembling parties to gamble and get drunk'. Gun clubs sprang up all over the country, the most famous being the London Gun Club, known as the Red House, in Notting Hill and the Hurlingham Gun Club, called the Old Hats after the original method of placing pigeons under cast-off hats and lifting them up at the appropriate moment.

As the shotgun developed in the nineteenth century, trap shooting became an opportunity for gunmakers and cartridge manufacturers to demonstrate and advertise their latest inventions. The best shots of the day were enticed along to aid publicity – Lords de Grey and Walsingham, Dhuleep Singh, Lord Hill, Captain Shelley, Berkeley Lucy and many others. By 1875 the first 'inanimate birds' appeared. Initially these were glass balls filled with feathers but they later became saucer-shaped clays similar to those used today. As the popularity of these rose, so live pigeon shooting declined – aided by the disapproval of the then Princess of Wales – until it was banned in 1907.

Today there are 458 clay pigeon clubs affiliated to the Clay Pigeon Society, 196 of which are registered and can hold major championships. There are hundreds of others that are not affiliated. A glance at the *Shooting Times*' weekly national clay shooting guide will show sixty or seventy events on every Saturday and Sunday throughout the year.

Corporate clay pigeon shooting days that simulate a live driven shoot have also become extremely popular. They can provide landowners with an out of season source of income and help maximise the employment of estate staff. Recently I was invited to one on the Hambledon estate near Marlow, run by Purdey's in conjunction with the West London Shooting School. The school has been in the Richmond-Watson family for a hundred years. Guns stood at their pegs in the glorious June sunshine as every shape, size and speed of clay whizzed over us: little three-inch midis that were impossibly high, flat battues that curled infuriatingly just as I thought I was on to them, and deceivingly quick standards. Shooting was fast and furious, assisted by the school's charming instructors, who moved up and down the line offering advice. 'More lead on the high ones. Follow right through, sir. More than that.

Now you're getting them.' We had four drives on different parts of the estate and as a pair of red kites circled lazily above us, I probably fired three hundred cartridges using my old Dominion gun made by Phillip Webley. It shot as well as when it was first made in 1893, an accolade to British gunmaking which I doubt a modern continental gun could claim in a hundred years' time.

Some years ago my Uncle Ronnie gave me an exquisite .250 rook rifle made by Westley Richards in 1928. This had the calibre reduced to .22 in 1983 when .250 ammunition became very difficult to obtain. Since we were going to be relatively near Birmingham as part of our trip to Litt's, it seemed an ideal opportunity to take it back to Westleys to be stripped and cleaned.

Westley Richards was started in 1812 making good, solid, dependable guns, many of which were sold through their London agency in Bond Street. For fifty-six years this was managed by the legendary William Bishop, known as the Bishop of Bond Street. He was an imposing sporting character who was accompanied everywhere by two gundogs and was never seen, indoors or out, without his topper. Westley Richards have a remarkable history of involvement in the development of both rifles and shotguns. They assisted in the design of the first Enfield rifle in 1853, produced one of the first breech-loading rifles in 1858, followed in 1868 by a falling block mechanism ahead of Martini, and were involved in the design of the Lee-Metford bolthead. In 1875, their foreman and managing director gave their names to the world-famous Anson and Deeley boxlock action. This was further refined by making the locks detachable by the simple press of a button beneath the underplate: an invaluable innovation when it came to cleaning a gun, particularly on safari, where spare locks could be kept in a dustproof container and slotted in when required.

Westley Richards' survival as gunmakers who still manufacture the best 'London' guns is due to the foresight of Walter Clode, who bought the business in 1957, and latterly his son Simon. Gunmaking was going through a traumatic period in the post-war years and many of the great names lost their identity as they merged or were bought up by huge conglomerates. Purdey is now part of the South African Vendome Group and Hollands is owned by Chanel. Of the fourteen post-war London gunmakers, only Wilkes is still in the same ownership, and of the hundreds of Birmingham gunmakers, only Westley Richards and William Powell remain.

One reason for Westley Richards' continuing success is that they became leading manufacturers of highly specialised press tools in the 1950s and are widely recognised for the quality of their engineering products. The same machinery is used to make the components of the guns. These are then finished by the craftsmen on the gun side. Having a supporting tool-manufacturing business was of limited help in the1960s when there was precious little movement in the gun trade. However, when researching the company's records, Walter Clode

A double-barrelled rifle action

had noticed that the majority of their sales since the turn of the century had been to the Indian princes. He was astute enough to realise that, with the continuing reduction of their privilege and incomes, the princes might well be disposed to popping the contents of their vast armouries. These armouries contained an incredible range of shotguns, rifles and pistols by leading manufacturers going back several centuries. The elaborate engravings and embellishments often enormously outweighed the value of the firearm itself. Walter Clode was absolutely right in his supposition and for many years he travelled to India acquiring some of the most spectacular guns ever made and reselling them on the international market.

Simon Clode joined the company in 1987 at the time when there was a resurgence in the demand for handmade guns both at home and abroad. Westleys have very considerable overseas sales and have recently set up a showroom in Missouri to meet the American demand for high-quality handmade guns. Simon showed me round the gunmaking side of the business.

It was a fascinating experience. Here, David Lee, an actioneer, was fitting the trigger plate of a 20 bore, one of a pair ordered by the wife of a fund manager. Further on, Keith Hayes, a stocker, was bringing up the grain on a stock by delicately rubbing the wood with sandpaper so fine you could scarcely feel the surface. On a shelf beside him was a pair of stock blanks of deeply grained Turkish walnut. Each blank is worth between £500 and £1000. One American client has recently chosen eight blanks for a variety of shotguns and rifles to add to his existing collection of Westley Richards' works of art. On another bench, Royston Hall, a barrelmaker, was fitting the top strap to an enormous double-barrelled rifle, a .700 with the chambers reduced to .500, ordered by another American and built to his specifications. The rifle is unlikely to be used and will simply be displayed by an owner who likes to invest his cash in beautifully made big guns rather than anything else. Nearby, another barreller was working on the barrels of a pair of .375 magnum rifles which will go to a Saudi Arabian prince.

Simon Gudgeon, the wildlife artist and sculptor

In an adjoining room, two engravers, Vincent Crowley and Rashid el Hardi, were working on a commission for a Chinese client. Hundreds of hours of painstaking craftsmanship go into making a gun but the engraver's work can almost double its price. Using a tiny hand-held chisel, Rashid was gouging a deep, intricate scene of dragons and phoenixes fantastically entwined on the action of the client's gun. When this is finished, fine gold wire will be tapped into the engraving to create a stunningly extravagant scene from Chinese mythology. Clients can have whatever they want engraved on their guns, from the traditional fine scroll or deep acanthus engraving to the sort of fantasies that some American gun nuts want which would make the old engravers rotate in their graves. Each gun is the painstaking work of seventeen or eighteen craftsmen, dependent on each other to produce a finished masterpiece that is an enduring example of the gunmaker's craft.

Not far from Westleys, in a quiet backwater ten minutes from the centre of Birmingham, is a magnificent example of Georgian factory architecture, standing behind imposing metal security gates. Recessed into the wall above the front door is an elaborate coat of arms, comprising a suit of half armour, a musquetoon, a drum, a mortar, cannons, sundry pikes,

Birmingham Proof House

swords and cannon balls. It incorporates the royal coat of arms and is topped, rather incongruously, by a spiked Prussian helmet. Beneath this impressive collection of military artefacts are the words 'Established by Act of Parliament for Public Security, 1813'. This is the Birmingham Gun Barrel Proof House, governed by a Board of Guardians of whom fifteen are elected gunmakers.

Firearms and shotguns have been made at Birmingham in increasing numbers since 1640 and most were proofed at the private proof houses of manufacturers such as Ketland or Gatton. The necessity for establishing a proof house arose from the sale of trade guns to natives in the emerging colonies. These were mostly of spectacularly poor quality, as was the powder that went with them. Many a Gold Coast tribal king lost his fingers exchanging undesirable subjects for dodgy Brumagem muskets. Unscrupulous manufacturers made fortunes and in the process brought honest Birmingham gunmakers into disrepute. This damaged the city's high reputation for gunmaking and increased the value of guns made in London, where official proofing had been enforced by law since the seventeenth century. To protect themselves, Birmingham gunmakers lobbied Parliament and established the Proof House at their own expense.

By the middle of the nineteenth century, over a million barrels a year were being proofed in Birmingham as the industry supplied firearms for the interminable wars that were so much a part of that age. Military arms aside, up until the 1950s there was an enormous quantity of domestic civilian guns of all sorts passing through the Proof House. Shotguns of every calibre, humane killers for slaughterhouses and veterinary use, revolvers, automatic and target pistols, harpoon guns and many others. Today, the flow of barrels has dwindled to thirty thousand a year, a reflection on the number of imported sporting guns from countries with internationally

The Proof House Museum

accepted proof marks, the Forces sourcing their weapons abroad and the ban on the private ownership of handguns.

It was fortunate for Clarissa and me that in 1997 the Proof House Guardians decided to collate the memorabilia that had accumulated on the premises into a museum. Open to the public by prior arrangement, it is a fascinating historical journey through the ages of gunmaking, with specimens of weapons made in Birmingham ranging from Brown Bess flintlocks and harpoon guns to examples of inventiveness in cartridge manufacture, from ones that explode to those loaded with salt for deterring dogs. There is also a chilling Black Museum with innumerable exhibits of barrel bursts and those in a condition that would be likely to cause an accident.

The exquisite works of art on display are a far cry from the earliest guns. The ancestor of both the rifle and the shotgun was a small cannon, mounted on a long pole and fired by clamping the pole under the armpit, saying a brief but earnest prayer, and placing a piece of burning tinder or charcoal over the powder touch hole. The first mention of these unsafe and unwieldy weapons occurs in 1374 when Willliam de Sleaford, Keeper of the Privy Wardrobe, got thirteen bob for making eight of them. The barrels of these early hand guns were generally about five feet long and a German manuscript of 1411 describes their loading. Handfuls of gunpowder (a mixture of sulphur, saltpetre and charcoal) were ladled into the barrel, filling about three-quarters of the length. This was tamped down and a wooden wad called a sabot tapped into place. Then the shot – a lump of lead or conveniently shaped stone – was fitted practically at the end of the barrel and the tinder or charcoal got ready. Here the handgunner's confidence rapidly evaporated. The risk of a barrel burst was appallingly high. Unless a friend

An antique French 'hut' gun in the wrong hands

could be persuaded to help, there was no way of aiming the weapon, and the recoil was bound to send him flying. Until the clouds of greasy smoke, reeking of rotten eggs, had cleared, there was no telling what effect the discharge might have had. Imagine, though, the exquisite thrill of a hit. One can see the singed, smoke-blackened face wreathed in smiles, the eyes gleaming in triumph and the awful anxieties of only a moment ago forgotten as the gunner scrabbles about gathering up his equipment, strewn about him by the recoil, for another shot.

Improvements came in the fifteenth century with the matchlock. Now the barrel was fitted to a primitive stock, making it easier to handle, and the powder was ignited by a spluttering slow match (a twist of hemp dipped in wine and saltpetre) which was thrust into the touch hole by a spring and trigger mechanism. The next step forward was the invention of the wheel lock, a complicated mechanism which ignited the touch powder by causing a serrated metal wheel to spin against a piece of iron pyrite and produce a shower of sparks. For the first time, a gun was always ready to fire, and a certain Laux Pfister became the first person to have to admit he 'didn't realise it was loaded'. In his *Chronica newer Geschichten* Wilhelm Rem records:

> In the year of our Lord 1515... there was a young citizen of Augsburg in Constance who invited a handsome whore. And when she was with him in a little room, he took up a loaded gun in his hand, the lock of which functioned in such a way that when the trigger was pressed, it ignited itself and so discharged the piece. Accordingly he played around with the gun and pressed the trigger and shot the whore through the chin, so that the bullet passed out through the back of her neck. So he had to compensate her and give her 40 florins and another 20 florins per annum for the rest of her life. He also paid the doctor 37 florins and other costs amounting to some 30 or 40 florins.

I bet that clipped his wings.

Wheel locks were expensive and their mechanism delicate, so they were almost exclusively a sporting gun available only to the very rich; the cheaper matchlock continued as the soldier's gun until the end of the seventeenth century. Such was the novelty of these big boys' toys, some of which were beautifully inlaid with bone, mother of pearl and even gold, that target shooting became terrifically popular in early sixteenth-century Europe.

Some wheel locks found their way to Britain in the early 1500s and these, with the existing matchlocks, began to be used effectively on deer and the occasional bustard. There had always been a huge demand for winged game. The majority was netted, using a setting dog, a hawk or a kite to hold birds to the ground while a net was drawn over them. Partridges were sometimes worked up into nets by setters. Ducks were lured into decoy nets when they flighted in to feed at the edges of ponds and nearly all manors had a permanent decoy, a netted system of tunnels, into which wild duck could be lured by tame ones. Hawking, and the ceremony that went with it, was every gentleman's sport but the necessity when hunting birds was always for quantity.

The shotgun came into being with the invention of small shot in about 1525. 'Hail shot' was made by cutting sheets of lead into little squares and rattling them round in a metal box until they eventually became vaguely spherical. The shotgun's potential for multiple shot was recognised, but there were still huge difficulties involved in actually getting a shot at game.

Matchlocks and wheel locks were at least five feet long and most of them had to be fired from a tripod. Even supposing one had the strength to mount the gun and swing it at flying game, the gunpowder would have fallen out of the open ignition pan, obscuring one's vision. So the only chance of getting a shot was if the bird obligingly remained on the ground, and virtually static – and all this after a laborious stalk, often using a specially trained horse, presumably with its ears plugged, or a variety of other camouflages or decoy lures. Despite these difficulties, shooting with hail shot became widespread. It was extremely unpopular with the hawking fraternity, who regarded it as vulgar and ungentlemanly. 'Villainous saltpetre,' they muttered darkly at the mention of guns. Shooting lacked any of the chivalry attached to falconry and ruined their sport out on the marshes, where the noise from the early wildfowler loosing off on a frosty morning disturbed everything for miles. Henry VIII was persuaded to ban hail shot in 1549, an act which was universally ignored.

Dutch wildfowlers are credited with inventing the flintlock at the beginning of the seventeenth century. These early 'snap haunces' used a flint to create a spark, but had little advantage over wheel locks except that they were cheaper. However, improvements to the striking action created a system where the flange could be used both as a cover to keep the powder dry and also, when lifted just prior to the shot, as the steel to create an igniting spark. This enabled continental shots to do something revolutionary: despite the extremely long barrel length and weight of their guns, they could now elevate them without being hit in the face by the powder. Shooting birds on the wing, known as 'shooting flying', had become technically feasible but the idea did not catch on in Britain for another quarter of a century, when it was introduced by cavaliers returning from Europe with the Restoration.

The best guns in the seventeenth century were imported from France and Italy. These were lighter than British guns and far superior to them, but they tended to be expensive. Surviving examples of the work of the gunmaker and his engraver exist in museums to astonish us with the beauty of their lines and workmanship. The alarming frequency of barrel bursts – common among British guns and cheap imports from other parts of the Continent – impelled the Worshipful Company of Gunmakers to set up a proof house in London in1657. Barrels were tested by firing a massive charge through them and those that survived the experience were stamped with a 'proof' mark.

Until the mid-eighteenth century, both poacher and sporting gent shot in much the same way as for the previous hundred years. Shooting flying with heavy British guns must have been practically impossible for anything other than birds flying away and shot at virtually point blank range. Barrels were now about four feet long, powder was unpredictable and the acquisition of something for the pot fraught with danger. Most birds were still shot on the ground and for large bags the traditional methods of trapping, netting and liming prevailed, but hawking had had its day. Even with its limitations, shooting was more effective. Partridges were ideal targets because they congregate in coveys and tend not to fly unless they have to. They were shot in September, immediately after harvest, with the aid of pointers first imported from Spain in the fifteenth century. These large, heavy, slow-moving dogs had phenomenal noses and were ideal for the deep, scythed stubbles. When pheasant shooting began in October, they would point to pheasants in the wide hedgerows and clumps of uncultivated rough ground, giving the guns time to prepare and aim their weapons before the birds left cover.

Shooting on the foreshore

Two discoveries at the end of the eighteenth century led to the practice of shooting flying becoming the accepted way for gentlemen to shoot. William ('Brick') Wall, a Bristol plumber, improved the quality of shot when he discovered that molten lead poured from the top of a tower solidified into individual pellets that were almost perfectly spherical. Henry Nock invented a method of igniting the charge through the top of the breech, rather than the side, improving the speed and force of the explosion. This enabled barrels to be shortened and guns to become more balanced. In addition, Joseph Manton, that wonderful gunmaker remembered for his beautiful duelling pistols, invented the top rib, which helped to correct everyone's habit of shooting low.

Less ungainly, more efficient guns and improved shot meant that the wily hedgerow pheasants now became a feasible target, and spaniel retrievers, which had been about in one form or another for centuries, were employed to hunt up hedgerows. An immense number of quickset hedges were planted to provide cover for pheasants.

The infuriating problems associated with flintlocks – pan flash, caused by the long delay before the powder in the pan ignited the main charge, together with the open firing mechanism's limitations and sensitivity to the weather – were solved by the Reverend Alexander Forsyth, minister of Balvenie in Aberdeenshire. Forsyth was a keen wildfowler whose quarry were frequently alerted to the gun's presence by pan flash. Consequently he devoted the majority of his time to solving the problem. In 1807, after painstaking experiment, Forsyth replaced the gunpowder in the open pan with small quantities of fulminate of silver and mercury wrapped in sheep's gut, which ignited when struck by the gun's hammer. After five hundred years, the open firing mechanism was about to become obsolete. Various people, including the ubiquitous Colonel Hawker, experimented with Forsyth's revolutionary replacement of the open flintlock mechanism, leading ultimately to the invention of the copper percussion cap – fulminate encased in copper. This detonating cap, which completely changed the nature of firearms, is still used today. Every cartridge, shell and bullet that is fired goes bang because of the minister of Balvenie.

At about the time the percussion cap was being perfected, J. Rigby of Dublin was among the first gunmakers to start forging 'Damascus Twist' barrels, twisting a mixture of iron and steel round a mandril to create light, beautifully patterned barrels. By the 1830s, shots now had sporting double-barrelled guns that shot hard and fast. For the first time they could shoot at birds flying at any angle with a reasonable degree of success. Shooting became a social occasion. The days of the solitary gun walking up with his brace of pointers after partridges were replaced by shooting parties. Pheasants began to replace partridges as the most popular game bird. Hand rearing, rigorous conserving and vermin control, to the fury of the hunting community, became the norm. Battue shooting was now the popular sport, with guns and beaters walking in line through cover, with birds shot early and going forward. In East Anglia and the adjoining counties, attempts were made to make battue shooting more interesting by planting circular pheasant-holding coverts. The shape of the covert caused birds to fly round and back over the guns, an early experiment in driven shooting.

Driven shooting as we know it today was the result of the next major innovation in gun design. At the Great Exhibition of 1851, the Paris gunmaker Lefaucheux displayed a gun which was broken and loaded at the breech rather than, as all previous guns had been, at the muzzle. Another Frenchman, Houllier, developed a cartridge that fitted into the barrels, which now opened downwards. This breech-opening gun and Houllier's gas-tight cartridge, the pin fire, detonated by a hammer striking a pin that protruded from the cartridge and was connected to an internal percussion cap of fulminate, was to send British gunmakers into a fever of activity, competition and invention.

Joseph Lang was the first to improve Lefaucheux's action but all the other first-class gunmakers – Manton, Purdey, Westley Richards, Boss, Lancaster, Woodward, Moore and in Scotland MacNaughton, to name only a very few – were busy employing the versatility and creativity in precision engineering that personified the great age of British gunmaking. Cartridges became centre fire, hammers became an internal part of the action. Ejectors were developed, smokeless nitro powder replaced black powder. Steel replaced Damascus barrels. Chokes were the topic of endless debate. It was a period of ceaseless ingenuity and

Goose fighting c. 1880

technological improvement. By 1900 the modern shotgun had, to all intents and purposes, reached a peak of perfection in design and craftsmanship. Many of the best London and Birmingham guns made then are still in use today, their value increased by five hundred times the original purchase price.

Lefaucheux's breech-loading mechanism enabled guns to shoot and reload at speeds previously unimaginable. A succession of high, fast-flying birds coming towards guns were for the first time within the capabilities of a competent shot. Driven shooting became all the rage during the latter part of the nineteenth century, with acres of covert planted to provide high sporting birds. Regrettably it was also a period of disgraceful competitiveness among guns and estate owners to achieve record bags, many of which were reprehensible.

Retrievers now completely usurped pointers and setters as gundogs, since beaters were used to drive the birds forward. The two types of Newfoundland, the St Johns and the Labrador, originally employed by fishermen in eastern Canada to haul nets out to sea and back to the boat, had been in use since the beginning of the century, particularly by wildfowlers. Hawker had one of which he was particularly fond. The Labrador's wonderful nose and steady nature soon earned it the reputation, maintained to this day, as the perfect retriever.

Periodically throughout the summer and autumn Clarrie would come down to the farm from Edinburgh, bringing her new acquisition with her, and have a bang at some clays. The howls of glee became more frequent as she began to get her eye in and clays that had hitherto sailed over her unscathed dissolved into clouds of powdery dust. Like many sports, if the basic co-ordination is there, success really depends on practice.

Towards the end of September we had a go at the mallard flighting into the old mill pond above the steading and, when it was too dark to see any more, tramped back to the farm with a brace of these delicious birds between us. As winter approached, Clarrie happily assembled the various odds and ends required on a day's shooting: a gun slip lined with wool, a large canvas and leather cartridge bag, cashmere shooting socks, mitts and a conical leather hat lined with rabbitskin, of the type worn by Attila the Hun on chilly days.

We had been planning a few days' wildfowling in Norfolk with our old friends, the Wells Wildfowlers, and possibly a visit to John Butler, a wildfowler living near Scunthorpe who has the unique ability to attract pinkfeet geese to him by imitating their call. Then we received an invitation for a day's shooting at Sutton Bridge in Lincolnshire. This was particularly exciting, since the Sutton Bridge shoot was the joint runner-up in the Purdey Game and Conservation Award in 2000, and their wild fenland pheasants have a legendary reputation for speed and guile.

Sutton Bridge is on the banks of the River Nene, at the edge of a glorious wilderness of marshes between the Great Ouse and the River Welland with the Wash as their northern boundary. It is an area immortalised in hundreds of books and articles on wildfowling. Between Sutton Bridge and the neighbouring village of Gedney Drove End lies a five-thousand-acre estate of prime agricultural land growing vegetables, grain, soft fruit and daffodils, farmed by more than forty tenants. Until twelve years ago, when Michael Gent and then later Alan Rogers, two of the tenant farmers, started to organise a cohesive method of game management, parts of the estate were overrun with pheasants and ground game while others were shot out by October. Today it is a highly organised shoot which involves all the tenants who are interested, whether they shoot or not. As there are no shooting rents and all the birds are wild, there are virtually no costs and the proceeds from the sale of game are ploughed back into the community in whatever manner a committee made up of both shooting and non-shooting members considers most appropriate. In any community there is never any shortage of deserving causes in need of funding. Donations have been given to local groups including the Scouts and Riding for the Disabled as well as the air ambulance. One year the playgroup was sponsored on a trip to Legoland, and the local pensioners were given an oven-ready pheasant.

Throughout the estate there is a concerted conservation effort in which all the tenants take part. The whole area is criss-crossed by deep drainage ditches which provide some of the game cover. These have to be kept free of rushes but, to provide a habitat for pheasants as well as a variety of little marshland birds, farmers on the estate cut either each slope of the drainage ditches on alternate years or only the bottom three feet, leaving the upper slopes for cover. Blocks of kale and maize pheasant cover are planted annually, and small spinneys that were established some fifteen years ago are now coming to maturity. They provide excellent overwintering places for many birds, as well as nesting cover in the summer.

Shooting doesn't start until late November, and by then the marsh pheasants are at the

High, wide and curving

Picking up

peak of fitness. Late autumn in this area is bitterly cold, in a way that is unique to the exposed east coast, and a vicious wind snarling unimpeded straight from Siberia cut through my tweeds as we joined the other guns for the walk out to the first drive. Anyone used to normal covert shooting would be amazed at the view presented by this massively flat landscape and the mesmerisingly vast horizon dotted with ragged grey clouds. In the distance, big skeins of geese could be seen ribboning the sky, with the constant tangy smell and sibilant sound of the sea in the background.

Shifting my weight from foot to foot to keep the circulation moving, I was letting my mind play over the history of the Fens and the great oak fire surround in the hall at my parents' farm in Sussex said to have been carved in exchange for a meal and a night's lodging by seventeenth-century Dutch drainers travelling back to Holland, when someone shouted, 'Over.' A cock pheasant, its tail curling in the wind, was climbing vertically over the guns at a height and speed I would have considered beyond the reach of mortal man. Breathing a silent prayer of thanks that it was nowhere near me, I was flabbergasted to see the gun three down on my left laconically swing up and tumble the bird out of the sky. From then on, while the beaters tapped towards a strip of kale game cover, all thoughts of Dutch drainers and the numbing cold were replaced by frantic adrenalin-pumping concentration as thirty-odd pheasants broke cover over the next few minutes. Like the fenland folk, these wild birds are fiercely independent and, gaining height at incredible speed, would hurtle away at an unpredictable angle. 'High, wide and curving' was a description that leapt to mind, along with mental instructions to give more and yet more lead.

Lunch in an old onion shed was one of those magical affairs with guns, beaters and picker-uppers eating together before we braved the afternoon drop in temperature for the last two drives. Walking back towards the cars after the final drive as the sun began to dip away to the west, I could see packs of wildfowl beginning to move about on the marshes. On a gust of wind I could hear the eerie hound-like cry of a Brent goose. 'This is shooting at its best,' I said to Clarrie. 'Completely unpretentious, all wild birds, and run for the benefit of wildlife and the community.' Clarrie nodded in agreement, her blue eyes bright with excitement. 'By the way,' she said, 'did you see the cock bird that went over me fifty yards high at practically the speed of light? The nice chap on my right said he thought I very nearly hit it.'

CHAPTER SEVEN

We Went to War for Wool

C

Wool, wonderful wool – there was a time when we went to war for wool. The Hundred Years War, with its heroic Agincourt speeches and all those rough archers giving two fingers to the French, was largely fought to support the price of wool. In the Middle Ages the fortunes of England were founded on the backs of her sheep. The gleaming church spires reaching like prayers to the Yorkshire or East Anglian skies to plead forgiveness for the sins of their benefactors were paid for by wool. In eighteenth-century Scotland, the horrors of the Highland clearances were perpetrated to make way for sheep. Today, what price wool – 50p a kilo if you're lucky and the wool is good.

Johnny loves his sheep, and if you use derogatory terms about them he will berate you. His hill sheep are brave and hardy. They live on wind and heather, and are magnificent mothers, but sadly their wool is worth almost nothing and their delicious carcasses little more. Heather lamb should be a luxury product on a par with Scottish smoked salmon, heather honey, or lobster, but it isn't yet. My great hero the Duke of Buccleuch, a man who has built a new abattoir in these troubled times, is trying to set up a marketing scheme for hill lamb, and what Johnny Buccleuch attempts he usually succeeds at, so here's hoping.

A sheep has to be sheared every year. A newly shorn sheep is not a pretty sight and one feels sorry for them if they have to go out into a cold, wet summer, but if a sheep is left unshorn, the old fleece sheds or tears off in an irregular way and the animal will grow a double fleece that is less weatherproof and more prone to fly infestation and infection. Shearing also helps prevent couping: a wet fleece becomes very heavy and if a sheep rolls on its back it may be unable to get up, and die. The Black Sheep brewery at Masham produces a very strong beer called Riggwelter, which is Yorkshire dialect for a couped sheep.

In normal years the farmer brings in a shearing gang who live in B&Bs near the farm and shear a thousand sheep a day. Shearing gangs provide a splendid opportunity for the rural young to see the world. William Dixon, son of Donald who you saw making crooks in the last series, did his first lambing with Johnny when he was sixteen and has shorn his sheep for years. He went to Norway to shear, fell in love there and got married. He has been to New Zealand as well, and still goes out to Norway for the shearing every year. Johnny always hires William's gang which often includes New Zealanders on what they call the Scottish Sheep Experience. They haven't come this year, because of the foot and mouth (which the Antipodeans take very seriously). Moreover, gangs working in the areas where the disease has been most prevalent have to work a week and disinfect for a week, so the work isn't economic since they're paid per sheep. They get 50p a sheep on average, half the price of the fleece.

We went down to Wales to see a shearing gang at work near Bala under the awesome bulk of Cader Idris. They were mostly boys from South Wales but the girl who rolled the fleeces was from the Falkland Islands. She had met a young shearer out there and followed him back to Wales. A gang of three shearers do a thousand fleeces each: three thousand fleeces a day is a lot to roll for love. They shear to loud pop music, which she was keen to put on as soon as we had finished filming. 'It helps the rhythm, see.' They had a kelpie with them, an Australian sheepdog which I have seen in Oz running across the backs of the sheep. The little white Welsh sheep had faces like cats. They are very small, and good eating. As the nursery rhyme says, 'Oh, the mountain sheep were sweeter'. Wales has done well for its lamb, which sells at a premium and until the foot and mouth outbreak was exported all over Europe.

The sheep are gathered and brought into large barns to keep dry for shearing. If it rains, the gang kicks its heels once the first lot is in until the farmer can gather some more and they can dry off. Wet fleeces rot and the mill will charge for drying them. Shearing is fearsomely strenuous work, and a young man's game. Nick, the boss of the Bala gang, was forty and muscular and sinuous as a polecat ferret, but he was the exception. (Back home in Scotland, Johnny had to hand shear some of his blackies for camera, and although he is splendidly fit and in his prime he was sweating up in the paddock by the time he had finished.)

The gang shear with machines and each shearer becomes very attached to his comb, which is plugged on to the system, but a good hand shearer can shear a sheep equally fast. A shearer controls the sheep between his knees and swivels it with his legs. Historically you sheared one side of the sheep and then changed hands and sheared the other side, but Godfrey Bowen, from New Zealand, developed a technique where you revolve the sheep and shear round it in a continuous movement. When Johnny learnt to shear in the late 1970s there were still a lot of people doing it the old way, but nowadays you hardly see anyone using anything but the Bowen method. This puts quite a strain on the shearer's back but does wonders for his thighs, which is why they are in such demand with the ladies. Johnny was just grateful to be still standing the next day.

I helped roll the fleeces. If you plunge your hands into a sheep's fleece they will come away sticky from the lanolin but softer by the second (which is why sheep men have wonderfully soft

Johnny shearing a blackie (note the curls)

hands). As I was going into the barn, a sheared ewe leapt past me – shorn sheep leap like lambs when the weight of the fleece is removed – and caught me on the knuckles with her horn. At first I thought I had broken my hand, but it was just very tender. I expected it to swell and bruise but after I had rolled half a dozen fleeces it was right as rain. Historically if you had broken bones they would lay you on a newly shorn fleece to help the mending process.

The rolled fleeces are put into a woolsack. The material used to make the sack has changed over the centuries but otherwise they are the same as the one the Lord Chancellor sits on in the House of Lords. Why, you ask, does he sit on a woolsack (which I can assure you is very comfortable)? Because the might of England was built on the wool trade. I wonder if the present Lord Chancellor, Derry Irvine, ever goes to the chamber and muses on what his Government has done to the price of wool. The sacks are rectangular. They are hooked up at each end and the wool is stuffed into the middle and worked well into the corners. Once a sack is full it is tramped down by a handy helper – in this case me, so it was a flatter sack than usual – and sewn along the top with string.

The lorry came out from Galashiels to collect Johnny's wool clip. It was driven by a huge man called George. The sacks are so heavy that they have to be shifted one at a time but George throws them about single-handed like children's toys. Usually he will go round several farms collecting wool clips from each before returning to the sorting mill, but this year he must disinfect before and after each farm. No doubt the extra cost will depress still further the wool cheque the farmer receives.

As we drive around the countryside, Johnny's eyes are forever on the lookout for sheep. He murmurs happily about the crimp in the Wensleydale fleece or how the Swaledale wool was always used for Arctic clothing because of the size of the medulla and the way it traps the air. He knows all about the proclivity of the Cheviots to lung disease when kept in barns in Newfoundland; the abilities of the Border Leicester as a sire or the Blackface as a mother; the propensity of the Southdown to produce fatty meat on turnips; and the general difficulty of handling mules.

We went to Stewart & Ramsden's woollen mill in Galashiels where they gather and sort the wool from all over southern Scotland and the Borders. The vast warehouse was full of woolsacks and fleeces in plastic skeps. The sacks from each clip are unloaded on to separate sorting tables. David Dewar, the sorter and grader we met, had been doing it for forty years. He unrolled the fleeces deftly, pulling the wool to assess the length. Fleeces that were matted or yellowed with sweat were put aside in one bin, poor incomplete fleeces in another. Johnny has blackies as well as Border Leicesters and each breed is easily identified by David. British wool is the mainstay of the carpet industry. It is fine strong wool, much sought after for quality carpets, sold to Belgium and surprisingly in large quantities to China. I am charmed by

Examining fleeces with the grader

the idea of dour canny Borders wool graders going to Shanghai to promote British wool.

Blackface sheep have one specific market, the Italian mattress trade. A bridal mattress made from blackie fleeces is supposed to bring fertility, so the blushing bride with her giggling handmaids goes to one of the special dealers who hang the fleeces on display for the brides to choose. I thought it was the Catholic church that was to blame for all those large Italian families and now I find it is the Blackface sheep after all.

The parcels of wool are sent down to Bradford for auction by the Wool Marketing Board. The minute a fleece is off the sheep's back it belongs to this government body which, since 1911, has been responsible for sorting, grading, pricing and paying for the wool. The theory is

The nearest I'll get to the woolsack!

that they will protect the farmer and guarantee quality to the buyer, but I wonder about its efficacy if they don't fight for the price of wool. Why, I asked, was the price so low? I had expected every answer but the one I got: imports of cheap wool from Poland and central Europe. Why, I pondered further, are we buying Polish wool when the Russians are buying ours? I looked for the board's website on the internet. Compared with the truly amazing Australian offering it was minimal, just telling the world that British woollen carpets are the best. It made me depressed and I'm not even a sheep farmer.

We went to Cumbria to meet a splendid woman called Christine Armstrong, who has invented a product called Thermafleece. This is a woollen insulating fibre to replace the glassfibre insulation which I fear may be the asbestos of the future. The wool goes through various processes, including a mineral wash to protect it from moths and other bugs. It is pressed and made into battens of the same size and length as glassfibre insulation, but there the likeness ceases. The workmen who were lining an old outhouse for use as an office praised the way it handled. There are no itchy dust fibres, it is easy to cut with a Stanley knife, easy to fit and excellent insulation. Christine's company, Second Nature UK Ltd, has employed a technical adviser who has had years of experience using fibreglass in buildings, but is now interested in breathable systems of roof insulation. She has spent three years working on the process and has received good wishes from the Wool Marketing Board, but little other help. Her partner is a fell farmer near Ullswater and she even has to buy his fleeces back from them at twice what they pay him. The fleeces have, to be fair, been scoured but then she has to process them again. Still, as he says, he has some of the last sheep left in Cumbria and he may not have them long. They are lovely hefted Swaledales, the pride of two hundred years of breeding.

Thermafleece

The picture is not all black. We went to Kirkheaton near Huddersfield to see Hunt & Winterbothom's textile mill. This mill makes some of the estate tweeds. For those of you who don't know, each large shooting estate has a particular tweed for its gamekeepers, a sort of livery. The design is registered and reserved for that estate. The colours tend to reflect the colouring of the flora of the area so that keepers from heather uplands will have a heather mixture and where broom is common specks of yellow appear. When we went to the Scottish Countryside Alliance march in Inverness it was a fine sight to see the northern keepers marching in their tweeds. All the patterns are kept in a locked book at the mill and we even saw the Balmoral tweed from the royal estates, which I thought rather understated. These estate tweeds can only be sold to their estates, not to the public, and the mill keeps bolts of all of them, awaiting demand.

The mill sells melton cloth (which is said to take its name from Melton Mowbray in Leicestershire, where it was once made). This is a heavy, dense, woollen cloth used mainly for hunting coats. We were shown a room filled with an array of melton cloth in all colours from ordinary hunting pink through Vale of Aylesbury yellow-green for the beaglers to French blue for the French hunts. The mill exports 15,000 metres of melton cloth each year, mostly to France and America.

Wool is for warmth. We would all be a lot richer and healthier if we turned off our central heating and wore more wool but, given the squeals of protest that my fairly cold house arouses, I don't see it happening. In towns it is difficult to dress. We go from unheated streets to overheated transport to offices where the windows don't open. In the country it is different. You are either inside or out and you dress accordingly. Bad weather is great if you are properly dressed. Last year when we were filming, the production team kitted themselves out in horrible artificial 'fleeces' and anoraks. When an artificial fleece gets wet it is useless for warmth; when wool gets wet the water takes a long time to penetrate and while it gets heavier, it also gets warmer. I have a vision of Johnny and me cooking on the beach fire on Mull. Me in my loden jacket, wool socks and tweed knickers, and him in his heavy 32-ounce tweeds, our clothes growing darker by the minute with rain but warm as toast, while all around us the production team stood drenched and shivering to the point of pneumonia. Remember, if you have green aspirations: wool is ecological, manmade fibres are not.

The problem is that you cannot toss a wool sweater in a washing machine. Cashmere is one answer to this, since it washes beautifully (and no, I am not doing 'let them eat cake'). Cashmere is wonderful: soft yet hardy, it lasts for ever, so is not that expensive in the long run. It comes from goats and is as light as thistledown before it is woven. I love cashmere. Isabel who runs my shop bought me a six-ply cashmere jacket from a factory outlet. It had been made for Givenchy but had a flaw and when I nearly died in Spain I came home to a Scottish winter and sat huddled in it for weeks, feeling warm and protected.

The Scottish Borders has a thriving cashmere industry, centred on Hawick, but we went to visit a woman on the Black Isle who has a breeding herd of cashmere goats. Scottish breeding stock is usually supplied by the Macaulay Institute who are constantly conducting breeding experiments to improve the fibre yield. The whiter the fibre, the higher the value. The goats are combed, not shorn, as the value lies in the soft second undercoat which is overlaid by coarser guard hairs; the undercoat is combed through them. The average yield per doe is 200 grams, though 500 grams is achievable, and the fibre from an average doe sells for about £30. It was strange to see the clip contained in half a dozen carrier bags rather than the huge woolsacks.

The main producers of cashmere are China, Mongolia, Iran and Afghanistan (but the Australian Cashmere Society is quite damning of Chinese fibre, which it says is contaminated with dirt, lice and coloured fibres, and of inconsistent length). The Americans recently imposed a ban on our cashmere because we would not abandon the West Indian banana for their Puerto Rican allies, and so ruined several small producers in the Borders. Happily the ban has now been lifted, and the price of British cashmere is quite strong at the moment because the Mongolians, who are the world's main suppliers, had a bad season which wiped out their flocks.

One of the advantages of cashmere goats is that they will graze out the unwanted weeds in a field and even eat leafy spurge. The disadvantage is the smell, which, while not so bad as some breeds, is quite noticeable. Cashmere goats do well where there are cold winters and this can be a problem for British suppliers. A trend to cashmere back in the 1980s went badly wrong and Johnny found three cashmere goats running loose on his hill. He caught them up and gave them to the man who was collecting the wool clip. Two ended up as meat but the third was adopted as a pet and pulled a little goat cart for a child. The recent craze for cashmere pashminas gave a strong boost to the market, which will no doubt drop back, but this is an interesting diversification.

From looking at one of the lightest fabrics, Johnny and I went to investigate one of the heaviest, Harris Tweed, made on the Isle of Lewis. Tweedmaking is one of the main industries of Harris, Lewis, Benbecula, and one or two other small islands. Harris Tweed is woven from virgin wool, spun in mills on the island and handwoven at home by weavers in the old traditional way. When the Harris Tweed orb mark was first registered in 1909 the wool had to be handspun by the weavers. After an extremely long court case, the Harris Tweed Act of 1963 regularised the weaving and allowed mill yarn to be used.

Harris Tweed owes much of its popularity to an English woman called Lady Dunmore, who first made it fashionable at the end of the nineteenth century. When she came across it in 1896, she found a heavy, hard-wearing material, that was thornproof, virtually waterproof and perfect for stalking and shooting clothing. I can remember the very distinctive smell of my father's tweeds, made up as it was of the scent of the cottagers' peat fires and what I later discovered was the urine in which the cloth was soaked. In wet weather a group of shooting gentlemen could smell very ripe indeed. It was rough, hairy stuff which needed to be worn for years in bad weather before it was properly broken in and weighed the equivalent of 36 ounces to the yard at full width.

Lady Dunmore's friends in the gentry made Harris Tweed the *dernier cri* of shooting circles in the early twentieth century (and it is still ideal for sporting clothes) but in the 1960s the tweed suddenly became the stuff of high fashion, being worn by Hollywood stars and foreign millionaires as well as traditional country gentlemen. Those were heady days, with three million metres a year leaving the islands. As so often happens, the tweedmakers devalued their own product by allowing it to be sold in discount shops in America and destroying its luxury image. Today only one million metres a year are sold. We visited the tweed mill and admired the lighter tweeds woven to the designs of fashion luminaries such as Jean Paul Gaultier, John Galliano and Vivienne Westwood, but these are not available to the general public and the other designs are for the most part ugly and synthetic-looking. The older sporting tweeds still hold up but I, who had gone intending to buy a couple of bolts, found nothing I wanted.

Until we went to Breanish Tweeds. What joy! The finest tweeds on the island are being produced by Ian Sutherland, a retired superintendent of the Ugandan police force who returned to his native Lewis and became bored with retirement. Driving the school bus and general crofting didn't fill the gap, so at a friend's suggestion he bought a loom. He weaves cashmere, silk and lambswool through his cloth and has a splendid eye for colour and design. He bears his own label because he doesn't want to weave the designs imposed on the weavers by the mill and the Harris Tweed Authority, and sells to Anderson & Sheppard (Johnny's London tailors) in the UK, and to overseas customers in Austria, Germany, Switzerland and the United States. When we arrived he had just received a large order from a leading US tailor who supplies garments to upmarket American stores. Here I remembered the lovely tweeds my mother and grandmother wore and got out my wallet with glee. This is the sort of attitude the island needs to revitalise the industry. The funny thing is that when he started he didn't know that his grandmother had been a renowned weaver! So at the age of sixty-five he has a whole new horizon, which is just as well: they are long-lived in the islands. Clutching my lovely jacket length and a large scarf for Johnny's wife, Mary, I headed happily south to watch Johnny heft sheep.

Over the years I have acquired a lot of knowledge about hefting. I realised this as I was explaining it to Nicholas Parsons in the reception area of BBC Edinburgh. It comes, of course,

Hoorah for Breanish Tweeds!

from spending so much time in the company of the greatest living expert on hefting, Sir John Scott of Beauclerc, aka Johnny. Johnny on hefting mesmerises audiences of rough farmers, pretty women, grubby children and even media types. For those of you who don't know, hefting is a means of maintaining sheep on rough hill ground which prevents them eating out all the good grazing first off and starving to death. It also makes use of the hill sheep's wild animal instinct to retreat to the high ground at night to escape predators and return to the valley bottoms by day for water and better nosh. This daily movement up and down the hill is known as their 'rake'.

In the eighteenth century, the age of the golden hoof when wool was at a premium and more grazing land was needed, the graziers started putting sheep on the poorer hill areas. They had first to estimate how many sheep a particular area of land could sustain without damaging the delicate hill herbage. Then, in order to stop sheep straying off these areas or 'hefts', which were not fenced, they had shepherds living with the flocks at all times, moving them up and down the slopes within their own area each day. Ewe lambs born into this routine were kept in the flock and older ewes sold out every five years, so a flock was raised that automatically hefted to its own bit of hill. Sheep are naturally territorial animals, and today the shepherd's part in hefting is simply to chivvy them up in their rake, making sure they keep to their usual hereditary patterns, with his dog, his stick and even his quad for tools (unless some large friend has ridden off on it).

Like many other hill flocks, the hefted sheep on Johnny's farm are the direct descendants of those established there some three hundred years ago. The foot and mouth has killed off huge numbers of hefted sheep and while Mr Blair promises that he will reheft the affected areas, there is a shortage of shepherds, the process would require a minimum of fifteen years per heft and cost the taxpayer a fortune. The misuse of the headage payment may have led to there being too many sheep in certain areas, but the absence of sheep on wild upland will result in a speedy return to waste.

CHAPTER EIGHT

The Roxburghshire Rocket

In the middle of January last winter, on a lovely clear morning after a night of frost just beginning to melt in the thin wintry sunshine, Clarissa and I decided to have a day's ferreting. We took down the purse nets wrapped around their wooden stakes from the hooks in my workshop and packed them into the old game bag, then found the spade with the little blade I use when rabbiting and put a handful of sawdust into Fido's wooden travelling box.

Fido is a hob polecat ferret, hob being the male of the species, and my next job was to open the lid of his sleeping compartment and transfer him to the travelling box. Fido lives in a cub – a cage six feet long connected by a tube to his games area, another cage with a couple of plastic balls to push around, a small tree branch to climb on and a hammock to have a little zizz in when he tires of these simple amusements. His sleeping compartment is reached by a sloping ladder and during the day he is generally asleep, deep in his nest of hay. Ferrets are largely nocturnal and it seemed a shame to wake him up, but as I raised the lid and squeaked through pursed lips, there was a rustling and his triangular brown and yellow face thrust through the

Johnny with Fido

hay, his little rounded ears cocked forward and his agate eyes gleaming alertly.

Half an hour later I stopped the quad and Clarrie and I began to walk quietly towards a deep cleugh or small glen. I love this place. At its top end, where the heather and bracken are replaced by a rocky outcrop, Roman centurions once stood gazing north, searching the distance for gangs of marauding Picts. Up the length that lies into the morning sun there are four or five rabbit warrens, a badger sett and, further in among a patch of gorse, a fox earth. I chose a warren low down the cleugh where it widens out so that Clarrie could get a good view of the action.

Leaving her sitting happily in the sunshine on her portable stool, looking at the breathtaking views of the snow-dusted Cheviots, I started setting the purse nets. When opened, each net will cover a burrow and about six inches round it. A drawstring runs round the circumference of the net and is attached to a wooden peg forced into the ground above the burrow. When a ferret is introduced into a warren it hunts through the labyrinth of underground tunnels. Rabbits fleeing their historic enemy bolt out of their many escape routes into the nets and their impetus tightens the drawstring and tangles the net round them.

There were ten burrows to net and I worked with great care to make as little noise as possible. A lot of noise can frighten the rabbits more than the presence of the ferret and then they won't bolt, even though caught underground. When this happens the ferret will very often lie up with its catch, particularly if it is a Jill. Being female, the Jills tend to have a more primitive hunting instinct. From time to time, as I set the nets, I would hiss to Clarissa to toss down two or three more from the game bag until the job was finished.

Lifting nets

Now all that remained was to buckle the electronic bleeper round Fido's neck. Electronic ferret locators are probably the first modern innovation in the two-thousand-year history of ferreting and enable ferreters and terrier men to locate their dog or ferret if they become fast underground, by a signal that bleeps from a receiver box and indicates not only position, but depth. This saves an incredible amount of digging. Once Clarissa had buckled the collar I lifted the net aside at the topmost burrow, popped Fido in and we settled down to wait.

Ferrets are part of the Mustelidae family, which includes badgers, weasels, otters, stoats and pine martens. Where the working ferret originated is a matter of some dispute but I subscribe to the steppe polecat theory. Originally they were used to bolt steppe sousliks (the little central Eurasian ground squirrels) and marmots (the chunky rodents known as groundhogs in America), which were the staple diet of the nomadic Black Sea tribes. Rabbits originated in the western Mediterranean, spreading across Europe from Spain. When did they, and by association ferrets, come to England?

This is a question that has occupied academics for many centuries. There are those who vociferously maintain that the Romans introduced both. After all, rabbits were well established in Europe by the time of the Empire. The Romans, who ate practically everything, would have eaten them. They travelled with their living larders, and introduced dovecots, pheasants and the brown hare for coursing to Britain. It stands to reason that rabbits came over with them as well. However, Barrett-Hamilton, that great historian, crushingly stated on page 184 of his *A History of British Mammals* (1910): 'The supposition that the rabbit was introduced by the Romans is without foundation as it had no native name in any part of these Kingdoms until the Normans came over and named it.' What is more, Barrett-Hamilton played his ace by quoting from Dr Browne's famous *Life of Bede* in which he cites the evidence for the first pictorial evidence of the rabbit. This is to be found on the robes in which the skeletal remains of St Cuthbert were tenderly transported from the monastery on Lindisfarne to the recently erected Durham Cathedral. The robes are thought to have been made between 1085 and 1104, and have a border depicting a hunting scene of a horseman, 'with hawk in hand and a row of rabbits beneath'.

The Normans certainly established warrens all over the country. Rabbits were big business. Apart from their flesh, the fur was used to make coverlets for beds, linings, caps and gloves, and for trimming garments. Some warrens were huge places, fiercely protected. The rights to create a warren were gifted by the king to his nobles. Many were given to the religious houses. Lakenheath in the Breckland of East Anglia was set up by the bishops of Ely towards the end of the eleventh century and remained in commercial rabbit production until the Second World War. The Breckland area contained dozens of warrens, of which Lakenheath was the biggest, covering 2,226 acres. It was surrounded by a bank ten miles long topped with furze and was patrolled daily by the warreners. The warrener's job was to keep poachers out, catch the rabbits with net and ferret, salt the skins, and cut hay to feed the animals through the winter. Big warrens had fortified lodges in which the skins were stored. The remains of one of these still stands at Thetford Warren in Norfolk.

Inevitably, some rabbits escaped and were soon breeding in the surrounding countryside. Sooner or later an observant serf, watching the warreners at work, thought of copying them by

The end of a successful day

catching a young wild polecat, taming it and using it to catch the escapees. This was a risky business, since all rabbits – wild or otherwise – belonged to the landlord, and reprisals for being caught with one generally involved mutilation. Rabbits gradually spread throughout Britain and ferreting, depending on the vagaries of the Game Laws, became the sport for every man.

I adore ferrets and throughout my life have rarely been without one. I have had as much fun from a day's ferreting as hunting, shooting, stalking, coursing or fishing. But then, all of them provide the magic ingredient – a step closer to nature. My first ferret was a little polecat Jill which I acquired from an old man called Herb Bathgate, a noted ferret breeder and rabbiter who lived in a copse on the edge of the village. At eight weeks the kit, as young ferrets are called, was a sleek, writhing bundle of energy and inquisitiveness. This is the age for a sporting child to get a ferret and it is the ideal pet for learning the responsibilities and sensitivity required in looking after animals. Handle a ferret sensibly and you will never get bitten. Cross the line and you pay for it.

Like many animals, adult ferrets come in season and mate in the early spring. The kits are born seven weeks later and are weaned at eight weeks. Herb gave me the little Jill in the middle of May and I had the whole summer to play with her. I can still remember the exquisite pleasure of running down to her hutch every morning. My approaching footsteps alerted her and when I arrived she was already weaving backwards and forwards at the wired open front. I spent long hours following her round the garden, in and out of the shrubbery, as she pursued her erratic scent-driven explorations. When these palled, she would play endlessly with a rubber ball, pushing it about with her nose or dancing round it giving little cheeps of excitement. I was the happiest child alive and, after some thought, advertised my joy in the most significant way I could imagine. I christened her Diana, after my mother.

Old Joe Botting, our gardener, took me for my first day's ferreting in late October when Diana would have been six months old. Rabbits have no close season, unlike game, but countrymen give all quarry the courtesy of their breeding season. Apart from that, you can't ferret when there are young rabbits about since they won't bolt. This makes ferreting out of the question: ferrets learn the bad habit of killing underground and it is, in any case, against the nature of things. A rabbit's breeding season naturally ends in the autumn when the availability of food diminishes, but this depends on the weather. In a very mild winter you may see young soon after Christmas and ferreters, like wildfowlers, pray for hard winters.

I will never forget that first short day with Old Joe and the heart-stopping, thrilling thump thump of a rabbit bolting towards the net, the rush of noise and the grey-brown body bouncing in the tangled net. 'One'll do us,' said Joe, breaking the rabbit's neck and putting Diana back in the travelling box. 'She's only young. You mustn't sicken her. Now you watch,' he said. 'First empty the rabbit by squeezing her belly down towards her hind legs,' and a stream of urine squirted out. 'That's so you don't puncture the bladder and taint the flesh.' Taking out his clasp knife, he slit the rabbit from brisket to tail, pulled out the intestines and extracted the liver. 'Always bury the guts,' he said. 'Don't leave them lying about to attract carrion. Now you give her the liver and tell her she's been a good girl.'

Joe and I went ferreting many times together and each expedition was a lesson in field craft. From him I learnt the importance of silence. There would be plenty of time for childish prattle once we had finished. I learnt always to approach wild animals up wind so they could not scent us, and to watch the movement of stock and birds. 'There's a fox about,' he might say when grazing sheep suddenly flocked together. 'Thought I smelled 'un.' Or 'Something's amiss,' at a jay's furious chattering cry of alarm. He showed me how to set snares where the faint narrow tracks of rabbits pass below a fence and pointed out the thicker tracks of a badger. When there was snow on the ground he taught me to recognise the tracks of individual animals. The narrow, irregular hoof prints left by a trotting roe deer's slots. The unmistakable prints of a hare, with the larger hind feet in front of and outside the forefeet. The smaller, aligned prints of a rabbit. The pungent orange patch in the snow where a fox had marked, and the scattered star-shaped impression of a pheasant's clumsy landing.

Later on, when I was a bit older, Tiger my first terrier came with me. I taught him to overcome his natural instinct to attack ferrets and, if I was short of a net, to sit above the unnetted burrow. He would wait quivering with anticipation, his head cocked to one side, listening for the thump of an approaching rabbit, and, at that moment when a rabbit pauses for a microsecond at the mouth of a burrow, strike like lightning.

Ferrets have always been synonymous with the working man and many a hungry family has been grateful to them. Until myxomatosis devastated the rabbit population, virtually every village had a rabbit catcher who earned his living with ferrets and nets. They used purse nets like mine, or short gate nets set across a gateway in a hedgerow where purse nets are difficult to use: bunnies bolt down the hedge and become tangled in the net. Then there is the long net.

Long netting is a major operation that is rarely undertaken nowadays except in rabbit clearance, but it was a method favoured by poachers, in the days when poaching was profitable, because a big haul of rabbits could be caught. It was done at night, and the whole of one side of a field, sometimes several hundred yards long, would be netted with fine-meshed nets, 3 feet high and 150 yards long, supported by light stakes. Absolute silence had to be maintained lest rabbits grazing in the field were alerted. When the net was up, a long rope would be laid across the entire length of the opposite end of the field and then dragged forward, a few inches above the ground, driving the rabbits into the net.

In many areas, rabbits have become immune to myxomatosis and in some parts are causing immense damage. When the sheep stocks were reduced in the Lammermuirs as part of the grouse moor management, the rabbit population exploded. There had always been a containable rabbit presence living in the grassy cleughs and glens, but the fact that it was the grazing pressure by sheep that kept rabbit numbers down had been overlooked. Rabbits live in rough ground and travel to graze on improved grassland and young cereals, where ten rabbits will eat the same quantity of food as one sheep. When they were disturbed in the late afternoon, thousands of bunnies could be seen pouring through the fences from the arable land to their burrows in the heather. In a short time we also began to notice whole areas of heather turning grey as rabbit activity undermined the root system and acid rabbit urine destroyed the plants.

None of the ferreting, gassing, shooting or long netting had any effect and vast sums of money had to be spent rabbit-netting the fences where the heather hill joined the cultivated marginal upland. Metal rabbit boxes with tilting lids were dug in beneath the fences where there were obvious rabbit runs. A pin keeps the tilting lid rigid until rabbits are used to crossing the box. The pin is removed in the evening and the box emptied next day. A neighbour of mine was destroying a thousand rabbits a month, for which there is no sale. The commercial food market has never recovered from consumers' revulsion at the sight of myxomatosis-affected rabbits, so most of the rabbits that are eaten in this country come from Spain or China. Fear of reprisals from animal liberation activists has all but ended the fur trade, and even the rabbit glue used in gilding has to be imported from Poland. When rabbits do so much damage, not only in the country but increasingly along railway embankments and in urban areas, it seems ridiculous that such a valuable natural resource is wasted.

The shift in population from country to town that began in the eighteenth century continued apace through the twentieth century, and many of these refugees from the land took their ferrets and terriers with them, a tangible link with their past and a reassurance that their grim new surroundings might only be temporary. Ferreting has traditionally been one of the ways the urban countryman keeps in touch with his rural background and thousands of ferrets are still kept in urban backyards. Unless neutered, ferrets will have a litter of twelve kits a year and, partly because of this, ferret keeping has undergone a dramatic change in the last ten years. Ferreting is just as popular – particularly as there is no shortage of rabbits – but more and more ferrets are being kept purely as pets. There were one and a half million of them at the last count, earning ferrets the title 'Pet of the Millennium'. An expanding industry has developed manufacturing compound ferret food, health products and ferret housing, some of which is so elaborate that it resembles children's dolls' houses. There is even a fad for ferret fancy dress – started in America.

Like any pets, ferrets can, sadly, become victims of abuse and neglect. Some escape from inadequate cages, others are abandoned when they cease to amuse and, unable to find their natural quarry, wander starving around the streets of our towns. Most large cities now have ferret rescue organisations run by dedicated volunteers who catch loose ferrets, care for the sick and injured and, when they are restored to health, find them homes with responsible new owners. There are now nearly fifty rescue centres catering for casualty ferrets, and they hold ferret shows and ferret racing championships up and down the country to raise money for the ferrets' food and veterinary bills. Jane Bewlay, her husband Jim, and a team of helpers run one of these centres, which covers an area north from Blyth to the Borders, west to Carlisle and south to Durham. In an average year she rescues, cares for and rehouses over two hundred ferrets as well as organising the annual ferret racing championships at the Blyth Fair.

I was telling Clarrie about this as we made our way back off the hill, with a brace of rabbits hanging from the spade and Fido contentedly chewing a warm liver in his box. 'They have an annual ferret race in Blyth,' I told her. 'In aid of the Ferret Trust.' Now, if there's one thing our Clarissa likes it's the opportunity for a flutter. 'Fido,' she said, 'has got to be entered.'

A ferret-fancier's dream come true

Fido was up against stiff competition. There were two hundred and fifty entries from all over the north, many of whom I suspected had been in training for months. There were beautiful silver ferrets, polecats, black-eyed whites, albinos and old-fashioned ginger ones. Their owners were no less varied. They included gigantic, earringed Geordies with shaven heads, covered in tattoos; housewives, little children, and a surprising number of pretty teenage girls in revealing tank tops, sporting rings in their belly buttons.

Ferrets race down carefully disinfected plastic tubes, 33 feet long, over a series of sponsored eliminator heats. There was the Moses Brown Memorial Shield, the Boots Handicap sponsored by the chemists' chain, the Ferret World Derby and the North-East Championship. On top of which, there was the opportunity for a really nifty ferret to reach national prominence by beating the current *Guinness Book of Records* time for the fastest ferret, standing at a scorching 12.5 seconds.

The Boots Handicap Trophy

There are six entries per heat, and the handlers and trainers hold their ferrets aloft as their names are announced. Twenty-pence bets are placed and, on the starter's orders, each ferret is thrust into its tube and its owner hurries round to receive it at the opposite end. At least that is the theory. Some do romp home, but others get halfway, pause for a think, turn round and scuttle back to the start line. The winning ferret is the one whose tail first clears the end of the tube, and this was the cause of endless heartache. Time and again, what appeared to be a dead cert winner let its owner down by refusing to emerge from the tube. There was one gloriously memorable occasion when eighteen stone of Sunderland beer and brawn, a veteran of a hundred bar room punch-ups, was to be seen on his hands and knees pleading up the pipe, 'Come to Daddy, Lily, come to Daddy.'

To my astonishment, Fido hurtled down the tube to win the first heat of the Boots

Handicap, doubtless spurred on by Clarissa bellowing, 'Go, Fido, go!' This has to be a flash in the pan, I thought, but no, he beat off some very professional-looking competitors to win his next heat. 'What did I tell you?' crowed Clarissa. 'I can spot a winner, be it horse, frog or ferret. Did I ever tell you about the time I won fifty quid and a second-hand rickshaw on a frog race in downtown Kuala Lumpur?'

The mid-afternoon excitement was claimed by a ferret called Megan, owned by an elderly lady from Belford, that took off like a scalded cat and exploded out of the far end before her owner had time to get there. She beat the current *Guinness Book of Records* holder by one whole second.

The tension was unbearable for the final of the Boots Handicap. Could Fido, a rank outsider, pull off the hat trick? Had he over-reached himself in his previous races? It is impossible to tell where the other competitors are in those last seconds as you peer frantically up the tube. It was Clarissa's ecstatic yells of 'Yes, Fido, yes! The Roxburgh Rocket! The Liddesdale Lightning! Ladies and gentlemen, this ferret will be standing at stud next spring. Book now to avoid disappointment,' that told me he had won.

CHAPTER NINE

INCORRECTLY DRESSED

In the spring of 1964, shortly after my sixteenth birthday, my father announced that he was going to London. 'You can come too,' he said ominously, 'and get your hair cut.' Those of us who remember the lengths one went to in those days to grow hair long enough to feel that we were part of the youth revolution, only to be thwarted by authoritarian parents or the dictates of one's school, will appreciate how this pronouncement filled me with gloom.

My father's quarterly visits to London always followed the same pattern. They began with the nauseating drive in the ancient Rover, with its sloppy suspension and all-pervading reek of hot leather and oil, to Moon's Garage in Belgravia, where the car was left for valeting. Next we took a cab to Truefitt & Hill, the hairdressers, in Bond Street. After lunch at Wiltons, there were visits to various West End tradesmen who supplied his needs, depending on the season. Holland & Holland, the gunmakers, perhaps, or Turnbull & Asser for a shirt. His view of London was very prescribed. 'Never go north of Oxford Street,' he once told me, 'or south of St James's.'

On this particular occasion he left Truefitts and made for Tautz & Curtis, the sporting and military tailors in Grafton Street, whose trade mark was a fox's mask with a brush sticking out from either side of its jaws. My father wanted another pair of white Bedford cord breeches for next season and once these had been ordered he looked at me sternly. 'Think he'll grow any more?' he asked Mr Dingle, the manager. 'Not a lot, I don't suppose,' he said, answering his own question. 'You'd better measure him for a pair of breeches.' My heart thumped. Breeches could only mean boots, and the step from jodhpurs to breeches and boots had a sort of bar mitzvah significance in the life of a boy who hunts.

From Tautz we travelled by cab to Knightsbridge Green, the site of one of the old London plague pits, which to this day has never been built on for fear of releasing the deadly bacillus, and to Tom Hill the bootmaker. I had been here many times before over the years, sitting whilst my father was measured for the butcher boots he wore cubbing and after Cheltenham

Mt Hutchinson's emporium

and when we went down to Exmoor for the autumn stag hunting, or the top boots with their patent leather tops, the canvas leggings and paddock boots he wore on morning exercise, and a whole variety of different shoes. A couple of years previously I had watched, green with envy, as my sister was measured for her first pair of butcher boots. Now it was my turn to sit in the measuring chair, first one foot and then the other placed on a blank sheet of paper as Frank, the venerable bootmaker, outlined the first of the seven measurements required for making a pair of boots, which were recorded in a leatherbound ledger by Mr Ball, the manager.

Hunting boots are made of a heavy 'reverse tan' leather, known as wax calf, about five-sixteenths of an inch thick. Box calf, a lighter leather, is used for eventing and dressage boots whilst polo calf, about the same weight as wax calf but brown and unreversed, is used for polo and military boots including, in the days when they still wore them, officers' field boots, which had six laces at the ankle, and Greenly boots, which laced to the knee. Reverse tan leather is used for hunting boots because its weight protects the rider's leg from the knocks that can be expected in the hunting field, particularly with woodland hunting. Just as importantly, it has a unique surface which inhibits scratches. In its unpolished form the leather resembles waxy suede from the nerve endings on the skin's inner surface. Polish is worked into this using the tibia of a red deer, until the surface gleams like glass. Because of the leather's fibrous nature, any scratches incurred during a day's hunting can be rubbed out once the boots have been cleaned and the polishing process repeated.

The dress worn out hunting has been criticised as elitist but it has remained virtually unchanged for several centuries because it is still the most practical. Even if you can't get proper melton cloth any more, the 32-ounce equivalent is hard-wearing, virtually waterproof and keeps you warm if the wet does get through. A stock protects the neck (or, if you hunt with the Border, can be taken off and used as a bandage for someone who has pranged their quad). Boots protect the leg, and so on. Having clothes and boots handmade ensures that they last longer, can be repaired by the maker, and fit well. Comfortable, properly fitting clothes are essential for prolonged riding.

The craft of shoe- and, later, bootmaking is incredibly ancient, and those engaged in the art were prominent people in early communities. Shoe- and bootmakers have their own patron saints, Crispin and Crispianus, two third-century Christian converts apprenticed to a shoemaker in Faversham. Shopped by someone to the local tribune, they were tortured with their own awls and, leaking like colanders and sharing the same millstone, were relieved of their sufferings by being tossed into the River Swale. The Romans, not unnaturally considering the quality of their roads, took shoemaking to a high standard. There was a reversion to the prehistoric moccasin during the Dark Ages, but a resurgence following the Norman Conquest.

Shoe- and bootmakers became known as cordwainers, after the soft leather made from mouflon sheep and tanned in Cordoba in Spain, and formed a guild in Oxford as early as 1131.

It was after the Middle Ages that bootmaking really came into its own as a separate entity, with those dashing Elizabethan and Carolean thigh boots that must have been hell to ride in. As the countryside opened up in the early eighteenth century, people were able to travel further and faster. This, together with the expansion and development of our cavalry, led to changes in styles of riding and hunting, and the riding boot that we know today was developed to meet the need for a stronger, more supportive boot.

Horace Batten on a difficult mission

The Regency period was the heyday of bootmaking. Britain reached a peak of fashion and elegance in both dress and architecture, and tassled hessians of the finest leather were part of any aspiring blade or buck's day and evening dress. By the end of the nineteenth century there were hundreds of bootmakers in London and the provinces, with many more on the Continent and in parts of the Empire, particularly India, all busily engaged in making sporting and military boots of every conceivable type. Many wonderful examples of the bootmaker's art exist in attics around the country. At home, as a child, I can remember dozens of pairs of polo boots, officers' field boots, canvas and leather Newmarket boots with their bamboo trees, as well as hunting boots with mahogany, champagne or patent leather tops and beautiful ladies' butcher boots. Sadly, none fitted and they were thrown away when the family home was sold. A pity, since nowadays theme pubs pay a lot of money for them.

Hundreds of bootmakers went out of business as cavalry regiments became mechanised in the run up to the Second World War. In 1908, London's West End Bootmakers Association had three hundred members. Now it has fewer than ten. Of the great historic names like Peal and Tom Hill, only Lobb, Taylor, Schneider, Maxwell, Foster, Cleverley and Wildsmith survive, making elegant riding boots in almost exactly the same way as some of them have done through the reigns of ten monarchs.

There is, however, still enough demand for handmade boots to keep the remaining London bootmakers busy. They derive a percentage of their business from abroad: America has more than three hundred registered packs of foxhounds and seven hundred unregistered packs and no bootmakers, with a similar situation on the Continent. Twenty-five per cent of Maxwell's business, for example, is hunting boots, with the remainder made up of polo, military, dressage and riding boots. Outside London there are a number of provincial bootmakers still in operation. Davies in Gwent is one, and Mr Batten in Northamptonshire is another. These two between them make most of the hunt servants' boots. There are 203 mounted packs of foxhounds, staghounds and harriers in Great Britain employing 950 hunt servants, who probably require a new pair of boots every eight years or so, and 750 masters and joint masters. These, together with clients who hunt often enough to need new boots on a regular basis, make up the bulk of Davies' and Batten's business.

Clarrie's determination to ride was still at the chair stage when I decided to take my old boots, patched and repaired half a dozen times over the last thirty years, down to Horace Batten's to see if he could work one last miracle. The Batten family has been making boots for seven generations, of which three – Mr Batten himself, his son and granddaughter – are actively engaged at the present time. The workshop is in what must have been an old stable behind a pretty cottage in Ravensthorpe. It is an Aladdin's cave of bootmaking, with its examples of different boots, sporting prints and old hunting coats. The Battens make the whole boot on the premises although local outworkers do some of the stitching, and there is a lady who makes the boot bags in which the finished article is presented to the customer. The family makes about two hundred pairs of boots a year. They make boots for officers of the Household Cavalry, and a few for the mounted police. Most policemen buy their special resin-soled boots off the peg from Allen & Cresswell, but there are those with a high instep or a bunion or two who come to Batten's.

It was while Mr Batten senior was scratching his head over my poor old boots that Clarissa took the next step towards hunting this season. 'I would like a pair of boots,' she announced. 'But there is one problem. I've got a wonky foot. I can see I shall have a job getting a boot on, let alone off.' Clarissa's damaged foot, an uncomfortable legacy from an accident when she was eleven, and borne with great fortitude, was no problem to a man used to dealing with policemen's bunions. After some deliberation and a lot of measuring by his granddaughter Emma, Horace recommended boots made in the lighter box calf with three laces at the ankle to facilitate access, to be ready for the first fitting in four weeks.

Bootmakers have always had a history of mutual support, Horace explained to me, and these long-established links are more important today than ever before. All the bootmakers help each other out because they know that their survival and the continuation of their ancient skills depends upon it. Lobb, one of the most expensive of the London bootmakers and the one who attracts a large percentage of the international market, sends work out to bootmakers around the country, and if one of the London bootmakers is placing an order for leather from the tanners, they may contact the smaller firms to enable them to add an order which the tanners might otherwise judge too small.

C Riding boots must have boot trees, so when we were next down south we went to F. Allans' at Pluckley in Kent to collect the set that had been made to fit my boots. Allans' is one of the two traditional boot-treemakers who supply boot trees for Batten's, the other being James Dobridge in Battersea. Boot trees are made of beech and ensure the longevity of a boot and help it keep its shape. The bootmakers send the measurements they have taken to the boot-treemakers, and the boot trees to the boots. They are made in four pieces: a foot, a shin piece in the front, a back piece, and a wedge-shaped middle, called the key, which has a handle or ring that is pulled to remove the tree. They are a thing of beauty and I can remember as a child being fascinated by the ones that went into my mother's riding boots. She had these beautiful boots that were made by Peal's for her when she married at eighteen. She had difficult feet and the boots took thirty-two fittings. When I was a child she went to visit the man who made them. He was ninety and on his way out and he said they were the finest boots he had ever made.

Meanwhile, as we were still in the Midlands, I went with Johnny to see Mr Ripley at the world-famous Frank Hall's in Market Harborough. Johnny was having a pair of breeches made and, because of my vow to return to hunting, I ordered a new black hunting coat. This tiny shop sends bespoke hunting coats all over the world. There are splendid pictures of the late King George VI hunting from Windsor, and hanging on the wall was Prince Charles' coat, waiting to be relapelled. I have also ordered a pair of breeches from Mr Hutchinson at Westow outside York, another of the doyens of hunting clothes. I shall be so smart as I hurtle from my saddle!

'Suits you sir!'

A tree maker working on boot trees

Both these gentlemen travel the world making hunting clothes. They will set up in a room in a hotel in London, Paris, New York, Toronto or wherever, and take orders for a hundred or so outfits. They also make the hunting clothes for the hunt servants around the country. Each of them employs ten or fifteen workers in their local rural areas where jobs are scarce. To say nothing of the peripheral employment for people making cloth, buttons, leather and all the other appurtenances.

J What Clarissa needs now is a decent set of tack, a saddle and bridle, of which the saddle is the most important part. A saddle's primary role is to protect the horse's back by evenly distributing the rider's weight, with particular emphasis on protecting the backbone. It is essential that the saddle fits perfectly to avoid galling and, although there are some excellent ready-made saddles available, the best way to achieve this is to have one specially made or, in saddler-speak, built.

A properly made saddle will last for years and many of the ones in the tack room at home dated from before the war. On the occasions that my father needed a new one, he went to W. H. Giddens, the famous London saddlers in Clifford Street, which has now sadly ceased trading. Any repairs were carried out by Curtis Lloyd, the saddlers in the local town, until the local saddler died. Even by the mid-1970s, the mania for higher education had eroded the old apprenticeship scheme and, with no one to carry on the business, the local saddlery shop and its contents were sold up. My father bought all the tools and taught himself saddlery. I still have the round knife for cutting out and shaping leather, together with the edge shaves, plough

Saddlery tools

gauges, pricking irons, punches, spokeshaves, piping loops, tack hammers, lead mallets, wooden clamps, shoulder creases and awls, all wrapped in oiled cloth for the day when I can find time to take up leatherwork as a hobby myself. I even have the original blocks of beeswax, still smelling faintly of honey, for waxing thread.

At the end of the nineteenth century there were in excess of thirty thousand saddlers and harness makers in Great Britain, with probably half as many apprentices. They were part of a massive industry, making every variety of saddle in a world where, apart from trains, all forms of land transport were by horse. By the Second World War the motor car had reduced the figure to a third. Today most of the provincial saddle makers are no more and, with Giddens gone, Clarissa and I decided to go to Walsall, a town near Birmingham which has been the centre of British saddle making since the nineteenth century. Clarissa was keen to see leather being worked as we had been lucky enough to visit an old tannery when we were down in the West Country earlier in the year.

C We went to Colyton in Devon to see J. & F. J. Baker, the tanners. Colyton is a town which once owed its existence to the tanning trade. Like Walsall, it had everything the tanning industry needs: local oak trees, lime deposits and fresh water. In 1521 it was the fourth largest town in Devon and in the 1700s boasted two tanneries, three harness makers and thirty bootmakers. No one knows when tanning first started here, but the records show that the Roman legions bought leather for their uniforms and boots from tanners in Colyton. The tannery itself is wonderful. It is full of old beams and the 72 tanning pits certainly look as

The smell of the tanning pits is unbelievable

though they have been here since the time of Aulus Plautius. The 18-foot waterwheel which turns the bark grinder isn't new either.

Animal skins putrefy if left untreated, but tanning converts them into leather and so prevents decomposition. Baker's process sixty beef hides a week here (although the legislation following the BSE crisis, whereby beasts are killed at thirty months, has made it more difficult to find large mature native hides). The fresh hides are soaked in water for twelve hours to rehydrate them, with twenty skins per frame and each hide weighing about a hundred kilograms. Then they are put into a pit of weak hydrated lime for four days before being transferred to pits of stronger and stronger solution. This process takes two weeks in all, during which the lime plumps the hides, swells the fibres and pushes the fat from the flesh, preparing it for dehairing and fleshing (when the fat is removed from the flesh side of the hide). Any remaining hair is scraped off by hand, using a blunt metal blade over a beam, before the hides are examined for scars and cuts and sorted for use as shoe leather or in the saddlery trade. The lime alkali has to be removed to enable the tanning liquid to penetrate, so

It needs muscles to handle the wet hides

the hides are dunked in a solution of water and weak acid at 60°F for two hours, and then the year-long tanning process can begin.

To make tanning liquor, Baker's use fifteen tons of bark a year, which comes from coppiced oak usually grown on high ground or moorland and felled on a twenty-year cycle. Once the bark has been stripped off, the remaining wood is used to make charcoal or garden furniture. The bark is kept to dry for three years before being ground to finger-sized pieces. It is then placed in a latch pit (each of which takes sixteen barrow loads) and the sluice gate is opened to let the water in. Over a period of between two and four weeks, the water slowly soaks out the tan in the bark until the solution has reached the required strength and is ready to be pumped into the tanyard pits to start tanning. The bark that is left at the end of the process is sold for garden compost.

To begin with the hides are put through a series of twelve pits over a period of twelve weeks. The hides are moved each week, starting in a pit of weak tan liquor and progressing to stronger solutions. They are then transferred to one of the layer pits, where they will stay for nine months. Each pit may hold as many as eighty butts (as the rectangular central sections of the hides are known) at a time, piled up in strong tan liquor, with handfuls of oak bark between each one. Once the nine months are up, the hides are removed and allowed to settle for two days before the moisture is squeezed out and the leather is shaved level. If the hide is to be used for harness, it is retanned with summac leaf. Then the hides are set, using a slicker to smooth the grain, and dressed with a combination of mutton fat and cod oil which is rubbed in by hand. Indeed, virtually everything is done by hand as it is all too easy to ruin months of work. The hides are now set again, regreased and hung up to dry until they are ready for staining or passing on to their next process.

Baker's is a fascinating if smelly place, and the subtle craft of tanning has barely changed over the centuries. Good leather that is properly cared for will last generations. Incidentally, you may like to know that the buff leather which was worn under breastplates from Tudor times came from the wild Russian bull, of which Henry VIII imported a number for breeding stock. Chamois leather comes from sheep and Moroccan leather is tanned with dog excrement, which is one of the by-products of hound kennels.

J Tanneries came a little later to Walsall. In the Middle Ages it was the hub of the lorinery industry. Loriners were the saddlers' ironmongers and made stirrups, bits, buckles, spurs, the metal reinforcements for saddle trees, harness mounts and decorations. The loriners' chief requirements were high-grade charcoal, limestone and iron and the forests around Walsall and Birmingham provided all these materials. A number of curriers (or leather curers) established themselves in the town during the eighteenth century, working on high-quality hides imported from tanneries such as Baker's, and it was only natural that bridle makers should also move to the area.

With the opening of the Walsall canal in 1799, and the arrival of the railway not long after, the number of saddlers and harness makers began to increase. By 1840, there were 170 leather workers, but only one small tannery. Forty years later the number of craftsmen had escalated to 3,500, with nearly 450 tanners and curriers providing the leather. In 1900, 7,000 saddlers and a whole army of outworkers were making military saddles for every nation in the world. One company alone produced an astonishing 100,000 cavalry saddles for the British army between 1914 and 1916. There was a steady decline between 1920 and 1970 but now, with the growth in popularity of all equestrian sports and the demand for high-quality leather goods, Walsall has one of the highest concentrations of saddlers anywhere in the world, with 65 saddle-making firms and several thousand people employed in the leather goods trade, which ranges all the way from heavy-horse harnesses to menu covers, cartridge bags, gloves, handbags and briefcases.

The whole town of Walsall is in many ways a monument to the saddlery industry, with its proliferation of tall factory buildings, some dating back to the beginning of the nineteenth century. Even the rows of Victorian terraced houses, familiar in every industrial town, have a unique architectural addition: a box-shaped extension where the outworkers sat and stitched in the heyday of saddle making. The Walsall Leather Museum is a fascinating place, with displays of high-cantled seventeenth-century saddles and examples of typical Walsall-made military and racing saddles, as well as elaborately quilted ladies' side-saddles, gaucho and even camel saddles, covering a period of nearly three hundred years. There is also a selection of every sort of lorinery.

Wherever you drive through Walsall there are signs for saddle and bridle-making firms and many others for leather goods. One of the biggest and best-known saddlers is Jabez Cliff, the royal warrant holder. Frank Baines and Keith Bryan are two more that we passed on our way to E. Jeffries and Sons in George Street, a name I remembered from seeing one of their saddles in Giddens, years ago. Duncan Kent, chief executive of Jeffries, had kindly agreed to let us see a large saddle-making firm in operation. The company makes about two thousand saddles a year, covering the whole range of equestrian disciplines: polo saddles, saddles for the increasingly popular endurance competitions, dressage saddles, working hunter and show-jumping saddles. Like most of the Walsall saddlers they have developed international markets and this was reflected in the bridle designs: raised browbands and nosebands with decorative stitching, and laced reins.

Jeffries was an extraordinary mix of ancient and modern saddle making methods. Here a bridle cutter was cutting leather strips from a leather butt (the trade name for a whole cured hide) measuring 5 feet by 2 feet – one of an enormous quantity stacked in racks. Using a special cutting tool with a wickedly sharp blade on one side and an adjustable clamp on the other, the bridle cutter was deftly cutting strips one inch thick just as his forebears did two hundred years ago. Next to him another leather worker was levelling the thickness of the strips with a modern leather-splitting machine.

The long wooden-floored workshop was a hive of activity, with groups of women stitchers working on pattern-stitched nosebands and browbands using two needles with amazing speed. At the benches down either side of the workshop, bridle makers were using curved edge shaves to remove sharp edges from bridle straps before heating a tool known as a shoulder crease to harden and set the edge. Some were tapping pricking irons with wooden mallets, marking the leather with the irons' inch-long teeth to guide the hand stitchers, while others were operating electronic punching machines, which coughed out small unwanted circular pieces of leather, or heavy-duty sewing machines used for stitching long, straight seams like the edge of a girth.

A saddle in the making

On another part of the same floor, John Flavell, the master saddler, was working on a dressage saddle in black grained leather with padded knee grips. The saddle is built in three parts, starting with the saddle tree and steel arch that keeps weight off the horse's backbone. To this is attached the inside part, known as the panel, which fits the horse's back, and then finally the outside part: the seat and skirts. It takes an apprentice five years followed by trade experience to equip himself with all the knowledge needed to make a saddle from scratch. John was surrounded by fine examples of the finished product, which reflected the increased interest in riding both here and abroad. They also reflected the changes in saddle fashion. Nearly all of them had knee rolls, something you never used to see. The old school believed they made getting back into the saddle difficult if you were thrown forward. Some had suede seats and knee pads, and foam rubber is used in the seat instead of the time-consuming wool stuffing. These saddles are undoubtedly of the highest quality and beautifully made, but I am a traditionalist and I wanted Clarissa to have an old-fashioned hunting saddle with a pigskin seat and white serge panels.

Not far from Walsall is the suburb of Aldridge. Here, in a delightful 1930s detached villa, next to a garage selling Porsches, Mary Brown lives with her elderly parents. Mary is passionate about saddle making and even more passionate about the importance of fitting a

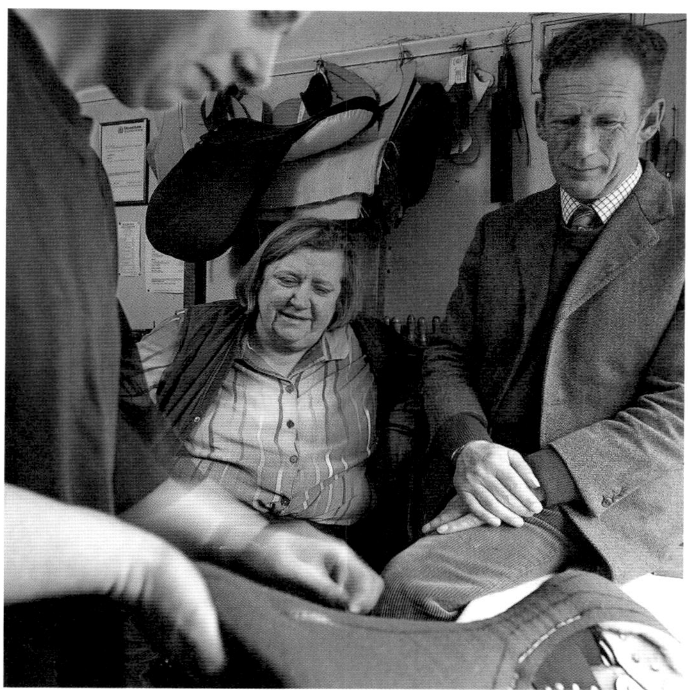

Stiching the seat

saddle to the horse. She, too, is a traditionalist, and believes that the saddle maker's craft, honed over centuries of making cavalry saddles, reached its peak in the 1920s and cannot be improved. The slogan on top of her sales brochure reads: 'When tradition has gone and fashion comes in – that's when the troubles begin.' In the spare bedroom, which she uses as her workshop, was the most beautiful old-fashioned hunting saddle with another under construction near by.

When my father went to Giddens for a new saddle, he took with him a template of the back of the horse in question, drawn by taking measurements of the saddle area using a striplead – a piece of lead piping beaten flat and moulded to give an impression of the spine and its curvature. As a cavalryman, he knew his horse's physiology well enough to give the saddler any necessary extra instructions. Mary, on the other hand, insists on seeing the horse before making a saddle. She then selects the appropriate saddle tree on which the saddle will be constructed. There are a number of firms in Walsall manufacturing saddle trees, which are strips of birch, laminated together and reinforced with steel. They make a selection of general-purpose saddle trees to suit various equestrian disciplines, such as spring trees made of thin strips of steel for showjumping, and will construct special ones for a horse with very narrow withers or a pronounced curvature of the spine.

A gent's hunting saddle was usually built on an 18 x 11-inch solid tree and, when women rode smaller horses their saddles would probably be an inch smaller overall. When building a saddle, the first job is to determine the length of the back of the horse and the width of the wither area. Mary will also consider the rider's height, weight, breadth of buttocks and the measurement from hip to knee. These determine where the knee will grip and where the rider will sit. Mary had reached for her measuring tape and, feeling that this might be a delicate moment, I shimmied off to smoke my pipe in the garden.

Through the open window, I could hear Mary propounding her ethos of saddle making. 'Before the war. Hold this end, would you, and I'll walk round. Blimey! As I was saying. Before the war, people going to hounds hacked miles to a meet. Hunted all day and hacked home. Troopers spent hours in the saddle. Unless the saddle fitted absolutely perfectly, it would ruin a horse in the same way a badly fitting shoe could. Nowadays people spend only a fraction of the time in the saddle by comparison and they overlook how vitally important confirmation is in choosing a saddle. What is the purpose of a saddle? Tell me that!' I could hear her demanding. Before Clarrie even had a chance to reply, she said, 'No, not to ride on. Its purpose is to protect the horse's spine from any weight.'

A large firm of saddlers, with many people working on the various component parts, can make a saddle in a couple of days. Mary takes a minimum of two weeks. She starts by tacking and straining webbing across the tree to form the seat, then builds up the shape and size from the cantle by stuffing the belly pads. The underside is covered in white serge and every piece of the high-quality wool flock, the size of a thumbnail, is poked through a hole in the serge and worked into place with a long-handled seat awl. Once the leather body, the skirts, serge linings, facings and wool-stuffed panels have been painstakingly stitched and fitted, the saddle is tried

Horse dealer Barbara Rich and head groom David Bland show us a classic hunter type

for a period, checked and adjusted. 'What matters to me,' Mary told us, 'is the horse's welfare. Not the rider's.' Her finished articles are exquisite examples of leather craftsmanship, which the great pre-war master saddlers would have instantly recognised with an approving nod.

C So here I am with all my clothes, ready for the horse with his snug saddle. I have given my statistics to the world, for the cause, and I have my breeches, my coat of melton cloth and my boots. All I need now is a hat. Nowadays people wear ugly safety hats and still get killed, or so it seems to me. I take the view that if your number is on the bullet, you have to go. Her Majesty is my great heroine (I wear pheasant feathers in my hat to show it) and she wears a headscarf, but she is a better horsewoman than me so I'll settle for a bowler.

Bowlers are a hard hat, an adaptation of the 'Billycock' named for the famous William Coke of Holkham in Norfolk, a key figure in the Agricultural Revolution, who designed it because he got tired of his top hat being knocked off under the trees in his park. It is named after Thomas and William Bowler, who were not hatters but suppliers of the rabbit felt from which the hat is made. Wild rabbit fur is particularly good for hat felt because it contains natural waterproofing oils. At one time rabbit felting was a major industry, especially when almost everyone wore trilbys or bowlers. All traditional hats except silk ones are made of rabbit. Historically this was the cheaper option and was initially used to strengthen the beaver fur that was used for hats. The fur is treated with a mercury compound which, if not properly handled, can send the handler mad (hence the Mad Hatter), and then repeatedly soaked and mixed with glue.

I shall take myself off to Pateys the hatters and buy myself a nice hunting bowler. I don't suppose Johnny will let me get one with a lovely vulgar curly brim!

CHAPTER TEN

'I WISH YOU ALL GOOD HUNTING'

When I was thirteen, I was interviewed by the headmaster of a school in Switzerland, of whose establishment my father had great expectations. 'What are your ambitions after leaving school?' asked this gaunt and scholarly man. 'I am going to be a Master of Foxhounds,' I told him. Today, all but the most enlightened headmaster would be less than enthusiastic about this response. In fact, in today's political climate, even the most precocious schoolboy would probably keep his interest in hunting to himself.

As it was, we discussed my choice of career in the light of its merits. Nor was there anything particularly unusual at that time about someone of my age, keen on their hunting, hoping to be a Master of Foxhounds (MFH). Hunting was accepted as an integral part of the countryside, and participation in it regarded as so healthy and wholesome that a number of public schools and colleges had their own beagle packs (as some still do). However, since his headmasterly duties required him to ask me more, I was obliged to expand. There was a family farming business in Northumberland, I explained, which I hoped one day to manage. My father bred hunters and he and most of my immediate family were actively involved in hunting and its role in the stewardship of the country. Several of them were MFHs. I had hunted since I was very small, loved riding and horses, and was fascinated by houndwork. Farming, the management of wildlife and the conservation of the countryside were all tied in together, I told him, and if a vacancy for a mastership came up in Northumberland once I was farming there, it would simply be an extension of land management.

Someone entering hunt service as an employee with the ultimate ambition of becoming a professional huntsman would generally take a job in kennels or as a strapper (a groom's assistant in hunt stables) and work their way up. The route normally followed by someone wanting to become a master would be to become apprenticed to a professional huntsman as an amateur whipper-in. A master and, more importantly, a huntsman would have to be found prepared to take on a pupil, so an amateur would have to depend on contacts. Those who are involved in country sports – shooting, fishing, coursing and hunting – are part of a gigantic network, bonded by a common interest. This is particularly true of people who hunt. The career structure within hunt service, for both professionals and masters, means that people tend to move about and they all know each other. An aspiring huntsman might start in stables with one pack, going on to another as kennelman for a few years then as second whipper-in somewhere else, gaining experience all the time. Even after promotion to huntsman, most people will make another move or two before settling somewhere.

As a small boy I hunted with the Old Surrey and Burstow (OSB) in that lovely part of the high weald of Sussex where my mother's family had lived for years and to which my father's grandparents had moved from Northumberland at the turn of the century. Both families had been actively involved with the OSB, my mother's father taking on the mastership with Colonel Robinson during the war. Jack Champion was Huntsman, with Jack Hickman whipping-in to him. There are many families with long traditions in hunt service and the Champions are one of the most famous. Jack had two brothers in the profession. His father and four uncles, grandfather, great-uncle and great-grandfather had all been huntsmen. Geographically their careers had stretched from the Southdown in Sussex to the Galway Blazers in Ireland, the Montreal hounds in Canada, the Zetland in North Yorkshire and even to Holland, where Uncle Tom had been Huntsman to the Dutch royal family. With connections like these, a good word from Jack would go a long way.

Jack was my great hero. He was a natural horseman and a brilliant hound man. Like many huntsmen he had a wonderful way in encouraging the young and I treasured his chance remarks to me. I was delighted to see both him and Jack Hickman, very old men now and following by car, when I was having a day on foot with the Old Surrey just after Christmas last year. Jack did me a great service when I was about twelve years old. I had arrived home from school for the Christmas holidays to find a new pony waiting for me in the stables. It was a 14.2 Connemara gelding and I was of course terribly excited, as any boy would have been. What concerned me, however, was whether my father, an authoritarian in these matters, would insist that I was schooled on him under the tutelage of Jackie, his then head girl groom. At that age, to be put over the jumps by a young woman was an experience I knew I would hate. The decision depended on my performance hunting with the Old Surrey and Burstow later in the week.

The meet was at the White Horse pub at Holtye. A fox got away quite early in the proceedings but made a beeline for the Hammerwood Estate near Cowden, a thickly wooded, rundown property and a haven for foxes. It was an awkward place to hunt hounds in, being all mud and overgrown coppice. By the time Jack got clear, I had become separated from the rest of the field and my instructions in the event of this happening were to keep Jack in sight. I saw him take hounds into a field, jumping a low hedge off the road, then cross the field and pop over a small post and rail into the copse on the far side. I followed at a safe distance. At the post and rail the Connemara turned awkward, as only a pony can, and try as I might I could not get him over the jump. I was beside myself. I could hear Jack casting for a scent deeper and deeper into the copse and then the lead hound spoke and there was that wonderful clamour of the whole pack giving tongue. Stuck on the wrong side of the post and rail, with hounds in full cry, I sobbed with frustration.

Eventually, turning back on to the road and hacking for miles in the direction I hoped the hounds had gone, I caught up with the field. I rode gloomily along beside my father, hoping he wouldn't ask where I had been. After a bit he said, 'Jack seems to think the world of you. Asked him if he'd seen you and he said you tried to follow him over a hell of a great jump into Thompson's wood.' 'He did?' I said, not daring to believe my luck. 'Yes. What's more, he told me that when the pony wasn't having it, he'd never heard such language since he left the Household Brigade. And that you never repeated yourself.'

By now we were living in the Southdown country where Bruce Shand and Ian Askew, old friends of my parents since before the war, were Masters. Roy Goddard carried the horn and his brother Derek whipped in to him. Roy had been with the Bramham Moor, and their father Harry was Huntsman with the Enfield Chase whose country runs right into the London suburbs. My godfather and cousin, Bill Scott, was Master of the Old Berks at that time, but had also during a lifetime devoted to hunting been Master of the West Waterford, the Portman and the North Cotswold. Another godfather, Jock Mann, was Master of the Vale of White Horse, as was my cousin Mason. In the late summer we used to go down to Exmoor for the autumn stag hunting when Colonel Murphy, Major Hambro and Mr Nancekeville were Masters. One way or another I would have been favourably placed to be taken on as an amateur whipper-in with a pack that needed a little extra help and with a huntsman long-suffering enough to put up with me for a year or so.

A successful pack of hounds is a highly organised, non-profitmaking rural business providing a service to the community. A hunt's income is made up of subscriptions from hunt members, cap collections, and profits from the major events in the hunting calendar like the point-to-point as well as the many smaller ones that are organised by the hunt supporters and foot followers' clubs. The enormously popular dances, quiz nights and the annual pantomime are all part of the role a hunt plays in rural social life. Its outgoings, apart from property maintenance, are the day-to-day costs involved in running a pack of hounds for twelve months, such as feed and bedding for the animals, hunt uniforms, fuel, and so on, for which they give the master an agreed guarantee. At one time, landowners provided the packs of hounds and paid all the expenses themselves. In the great days of the hunting squires – legends like Beckford, Meynell and Assheton Smith to name only some of the luminaries – fortunes were sunk into foxhunting. Indeed, until the last war an MFH would expect to make up the difference between what the hunt committee could guarantee and the real cost. Nowadays few MFHs have the disposable income to do that and in the majority of cases running costs must be met from the guarantee.

Like any other business, a hunt is formally structured. The hunt committee is the equivalent of the board of directors, and in many cases owns the hounds and the kennel property. Committee members are landowners, farmers and subscribers appointed annually, and fronted by a chairman who, apart from being generally affable and chairing the hunt meetings, has the responsibility of dealing with complaints against the master. The committee's role is to give the master every support in running the hunt country. It appoints sub-committees to arrange the annual point-to-point, hunter trials and hunt balls. The members of the committee are also usually responsible for the upkeep of the hunt stables and kennels. They appoint the hunt secretary, an often thankless and time-consuming post that is essential to the smooth running of the hunt. The hunt secretary is very often the treasurer as well and has the onerous task of keeping hunt accounts, managing the cashflow and paying the master his guarantee.

An MFH is equivalent to the managing director. He has complete control of the hunt and his word is law, both in kennels and in the field. He has been appointed by the committee and although they monitor his performance they should not interfere with him unless his conduct is a matter for inquiry. He engages hunt staff and they are completely under his management.

The size of a pack of hounds depends on the size of the country, the area hunted and the number of days they hunt during the week in the season. All these factors also determine the number of hunt staff. The Duke of Beaufort's, for example, hunts four days a week and has fifty-one couple of hounds (hounds are counted in twos), and the country covers 760 square miles. One of the joint masters hunts the hounds. When this is the case the professional

Moving off

huntsman becomes 'the kennel huntsman and first whipper-in'. There is also a second whipper-in. The Sennybridge Farmers, on the other hand, has eighteen couple of hounds and the hunt staff consists of one huntsman.

Every aspiring young master wants to hunt hounds himself and it is hound knowledge and kennel management that the amateur hopes to learn. You cannot hunt hounds (or work sheepdogs, as I have done for most of my life) without a combination of love and respect for them. With this must go a knowledge of dog psychology and that affinity with animals that is essential in all stockmen – and a huntsman is as much of a stockman as any shepherd, stalker, cattleman, ghillie or gamekeeper. The hounds must love and respect you, and look to you for guidance. Above all they must obey you. Like sheepdogs and gundogs, hounds are there to do a job. A master hunting his own hounds must obviously know all his hounds by name and they must come to him when called. On average, a pack will consist of thirty couple, so the names of sixty hounds, roughly thirty dog hounds and thirty bitches, must be memorised.

A typical day in kennels in the early summer starts at six thirty. The dog hounds and bitches sleep separately in big communal kennels known as hound lodges, which are sometimes of considerable architectural merit. Brood bitches (hounds selected for breeding the

Unboxing

pack replacements), their whelps and any sick hounds are checked by the huntsman, the first whipper-in (who is his right-hand man) and the kennelman, and the concrete yards adjoining the lodges are washed down. Then hounds are called individually from the lodges, or 'drawn out', and walked out in the exercise paddock by the huntsman and whipper-in. Any changes in hunt staff take place on 1st May and these early summer mornings, before the sun gets up, are a magical period when the new huntsman gets to know his hounds. At that time of year the pack will be resting before exercising starts again in June, and hounds are encouraged to play. There are grizzled old matriarchs and patriarchs to assess and become acquainted with, and shy young puppies, recently returned from their year becoming acclimatised to farm animals with puppy walkers, to bring on with a kindly word of encouragement. Every hound is an individual and the personality of each one must be learnt. A whipper-in's job, at exercise as on a hunting day, is to 'turn hounds' to the huntsman so that they learn to respond quickly to the huntsman's voice. Discipline learnt in the exercise paddocks pays off when hunting starts.

After an hour hounds are returned to their yards and any ailments dealt with. A huntsman, like a farmer, needs to have a fairly extensive knowledge of treating injuries and recognising

The hound lodge

disease. He may expect to deal with bites from fighting in kennels, damaged toes, and knocks and sprains incurred around the buildings. During summer hound exercise, much of which is road work, he has broken glass, thistles and the risk of inconsiderate drivers to contend with. On a day's hunting the potential is fairly wide. There may be eye injuries from working in thick brambly cover, torn or jarred shoulder muscles, or cuts from barbed wire. Some hounds might get hung up in a fence or trapped in a snare. There is always the possibility of a road accident and, increasingly, of hounds being injured in attacks by hunt saboteurs.

That day's feed, a carefully balanced diet of meat, minerals and cereals, has to be prepared. A foxhound is an athlete and during the season will be doing a tremendous amount of hard work. His diet is adjusted in line with his level of fitness. That glorious music known as 'cry' when hounds are hunting has much to do with their being in the peak of condition. Quite likely there will be a fallen beast to collect from one of the farms in the hunt's country. The collection of dead stock has long been a service provided by hunts which suited all parties. The farmer got rid of the carcass, the flesh was fed to the hounds, reducing kennel costs, and the sale of by-products was a valuable addition to hunt staff wages. The huntsman's perks were the hides and the rest of the hunt staff received the bones and fat, for which there was a lucrative market. A further perk shared by them was hound excrement. Until synthetic dyes ruined the business, hound excrement was barrelled up and sent to Bradford for dying corduroy. And why not? I bought a tie the other day in a rather jolly Paisley pattern. 'All natural colours,' I was assured. 'Those khaki bits come from that well-known feature of the countryside, the cowpat.'

In livestock areas, perks from dead stock were of such importance to hunt staff that a man might choose to stay where he was rather than pursue his career in an area where the flesh round was poor. Since BSE all this has changed. The value of by-products, as every stock farmer knows, has gone and dead stock must be commercially incinerated with charges of up to £70 for a cow or horse and £6 for a calf. To help their farmers, hunts continue to provide the traditional carcass uplift service. One I know, with a country of 700 square miles, collects something like 250 cows, 40 horses and 2,500 calves annually, saving farmers in the area about £35,000. Running costs for the hunt lorry amount to about £9,000. To install an incinerator to environmental standards costs the hunt about £10,000 with a further £10,000 annually in overheads. Paradoxically, in 1999, at the time the Foster Bill to ban controlling vermin with dogs was going before Parliament, the Ministry of Agriculture was advising farmers with unsaleable calves to apply to their local hunts to remove them. More recently, because many of them are qualified slaughtermen, a considerable number of hunt staff stepped in to help when foot and mouth devastated the countryside.

Midday, and the hounds are fed, shoulder to shoulder, at the troughs in their yards. The huntsman should always be present so that they recognise him as the provider. Particular care is taken to see that shy hounds get in to eat, and to watch for a normally healthy eater hanging back from his grub. Hounds are taken into the exercise paddock for another hour's educational play before finally being sent back into their lodges for the night.

During the evening there are the accounts to check, letters to write and an endless number of telephone calls to make. There may be fifteen hundred farmers in a hunt's country and the hunt is the focus of social communications in the area. Last thing at night the kennels and stables are checked again. In the case of the Old Surrey and Burstow, where they are under virtual siege from animal welfare activists, the chain link fencing with its overhead security lighting, alarms and smoke detectors must all be tested. Not long ago the stable block with hunt horses in their stalls was set on fire, and not far away an entire pack of beagles was stolen – only one of which, mutilated and confused, has ever been found.

As the summer progresses, the relationship between hounds and huntsman continues to develop as the exercise programme increases. There is the annual puppy show at the kennels to organise, when young hounds are judged by a visiting master or huntsman, and there is a party to thank and entertain the puppy walkers and the local landowners and farmers. Apart

Hunting c. 1935

from hound work, every hunt is involved in conservation and there are always rides to be cut back through woodland and hunt gates to build and repair. Visits are made to organisers of shoots in the hunt country so that their shooting days can be planned in relation to hunting in the area, and there is liaison to be done with other interested bodies like the Forestry Commission, various heritage organisations and the police.

Cubbing, or autumn hunting as it is now called, starts in mid-August or September, depending on the harvest. The word cub is a misnomer in that it suggests a small, cuddly, defenceless animal, whereas in fact fox cubs by then are nearly as large as their parents, are hunting for themselves and are, like adult foxes, ruthless predators. The object of cub hunting is to test the elementary training of the young hounds and give them the experience of hunting. Initiative and boldness have been encouraged during the summer months. Instant and willing obedience has also formed part of the training. Now it is all put into practice in the field.

A huntsman will concentrate on hunting in covert, giving young hounds the opportunity to learn to use their noses by keeping to the cry of old hounds and imitating what they do. Young adult foxes are still living in family groups; cub hunting disperses them and culls out the weak and sickly. A huntsman uses his knowledge of country lore in selecting which coverts to draw. Foxes like to lie up in woodland that is not too densely planted so that sunlight allows warmth to penetrate and ground cover to grow. They like an elevated position and would obviously avoid damp places. A tip I learnt off Jack Champion years ago was never to bother looking for cubs in oak plantations in the late autumn – falling acorns unnerve them and to a fox's sensitive ears, sound like footsteps. Hunting proper starts on 1st November and by then a huntsman will have wonderful power over his hounds. They will be eager yet obedient; stick close to him or seek widely at his command; hunt with the utmost determination but still be responsive enough to be called off the line if danger looms – and only one man in the world at that moment has the ability to do this.

A huntsman has many things to do while hunting his hounds. He must gauge whether it is a good or bad scenting day. Scent comes from body vapour and direct contact with the ground, and is said to be good when air and ground are moist; in a south or west wind; in the afternoon before a frost; and in long grass and heather. Scent is bad when the wind is northerly or there is a storm brewing; when cobwebs hang on the bushes; in harsh drying winds; and when the sky is clear, particularly on days when there is a blue haze; or in heavy rain. Scent is full of complexities, or, as Roy Goddard once remarked when we were discussing it one day, 'There's nowt so queer as scent 'cept, possibly, a woman.'

What has a huntsman to think of when hounds are running with a scent? He must decide whether there is only one fox in front of hounds and whether there is a likelihood of an outlier being put up. He must consider how far ahead of hounds the fox is in relation to possible

Fell hunting

hazards such as roads, railways, urban areas and parts of the country over which the hounds may not have permission to hunt, and the direction the fox may take. Here the movement of stock and birds will guide him: sheep flocking, horses and cattle with their heads up when they should be grazing, rooks mobbing or jays shrieking all indicate the passage of a fox. What chances are there of a check (when hounds lose the scent because it has become confused)? A fox is the most cunning animal on earth. He has been hunted by hounds for more than a thousand years and the sound of a pack in full cry will not distract him in the least. He will use all his instincts to disguise his scent. I have watched a hunted fox trot twice round a flock of bunched sheep before ambling on. They will immerse themselves in running water or deliberately walk through farmyard slurry. Last season, hunting with the Border, I saw a fox make his way to a fence line and weave between the stobs along a hundred-yard length before trotting off to sit and watch the effect. Hounds hunt entirely by scent and the pack followed it back and forth between the stobs. The list is endless.

When hounds have checked, a huntsman uses his knowledge of wildlife and the complex behavioural pattern of foxes to guess where he will have gone next. He must think like a fox and a hound at the same time. The telepathy between a huntsman and his hounds is very acute and mental energy plays a large part – as it does when handling sheepdogs or working gundogs. The huntsman's will to see his job as a vermin controller successfully concluded must be transmitted to his hounds, instilling vigour and keenness in them. A lacklustre huntsman will have lacklustre hounds and he will fail in his duty to the farming and landowning community.

The modern huntsman has other things to think of as he rides across country, searching the landscape and conserving his horse's energy. There is the piano wire stretched over hunt jumps to watch for, and aniseed trails and ammonia attacks on hounds to cope with. Many hunt saboteurs carry sprung steel rods for lashing at hounds or horses. Isolated in some covert, the huntsman and other members of the hunt staff may well be vulnerable to attack. At the end of a day's hunting, hunt vehicles may have been vandalised and they always have to be checked for incendiary devices.

Like any other stockman, a huntsman works seven days a week, fifty-two weeks of the year. The rewards in financial terms are negligible but there are still people in this world who are motivated by higher ideals than money. There is a duty to the countryside and the privilege of working with animals. For its own good, our wildlife has to be managed in a manner that is both humane and effective. Detractors of the way we do it have yet to come up with an effective alternative.

When I was thirteen I wanted to become an MFH because I would be following a family tradition which I knew to be important to the preservation of rural Britain. Today that role is even more important. 'There's many a slip 'twixt cup and lip', but the ambition is still as strong.

C Every day now since I made the decision to get back on a horse and go hunting I rise from my bed and spend twenty minutes on a machine a friend gave me which I didn't use for two years until I discovered it was meant to be a horse and is called an Easy Rider. Before that I have already spent ten minutes posting to the trot on a chair. I do all of this to build up the riding muscles. I hate the exercise. I have reached the age of cerebral activity, so what am I doing? At fifty-four and overweight, I sneer at my friends who go to gyms and take up running. I have a metal plate in my instep which some mornings renders me barely able to stand up when I get out of bed. Why hunting? It is over twenty years since I was last on a horse and I was never a wonderful rider at that. Why?

All the arguments, all the polemics, all the statistics about hunting were given in the last book. The book has been quoted as authority several times both in the House of Lords debate and in the Scottish Parliament. That was a great compliment, but what now? 'Tell them,' Johnny said. 'Just tell them why you want to get back on a horse and go hunting again.' I look around as I pedal away. My house is full of books. Every room has a bookshelf. There are books on food, books on cookery, books of poetry, books on travel, books on antiques, even some fiction that I have decided to keep and not give to the library. Beside my bed I keep my favourites: Dorothy Hartley's *Food in England*, Claudia Roden's *Jewish Food*, Alan Davidson, Theodora FitzGibbon. They are all food books bar three. Yeats' poetry is easily explained: I like a good cry now and again. But the other two? Siegfried Sassoon's *Memoirs of a Fox-Hunting Man* and Surtees' *Mr Facey Romford's Hounds*. It had never really struck me until now. The books were just there.

I sit at my desk and try to analyse my behaviour. I start with my family. My grandmother spent much of her life on horses. When she became fabulously rich after the death of her second husband, she would come home from Australia every two years to buy clothes in Paris and hunt in Ireland. It always seemed that visiting us was rather a poor third. My mother was another superb horsewoman. Somehow via a Belgian aunt she had been made a member of the Royal Belgian Hunt and had a habit in the beautiful, very deep purple that is their colour.

My eldest sister Heather was the horsewoman among my siblings. She showed her fine hunter, Sam Brown, and hunted endlessly. She was always trying to persuade my mother to buy her yet another horse because she loved the two-horse days of the great galloping shire packs. When hunting with the Quorn, the Beaufort or the Belvoir, for example, the country is so large that they bring up the second horses at lunchtime and gallop on. If you don't have a second horse and you keep up with the field you have to go home then. She was a great goer, Heather, and full of dashing stories. I remember her coming back roaring with laughter as to how, out with a strange pack, she had taken a lead from an elderly military gentleman who had led her across the largest jumps and the biggest ditches. She had kept trying to tell him she'd take her own line but he'd nod and say, 'That's right, you follow me, my dear' and out of politeness she had, until she discovered that he turned his hearing aid off out hunting and was stone deaf without it. She learnt to ride side-saddle in her mid-thirties off old Sybil Smith who taught the Queen, and thereafter hunted side-saddle looking very dashing indeed.

Everyone remembers their first day's hunting even if they were very small. Writing thirty years after the event Sassoon recalls it quite clearly and in words with which we can all identify:

> I was expecting an outbreak of mad excitement in which I should find myself galloping wildly out of the wood. When the outbreak of activity came I had no time to think about it. For no apparent reason the people around me (we were moving slowly along a narrow path in the wood) suddenly set off at a gallop and for several minutes I was aware of nothing but the breathless flurry of being carried along, plentifully spattered with mud by

the sportsman in front of me. Suddenly without any warning, he pulled up. Sheila automatically followed suit, shooting me well up her neck. The next moment everyone turned round and we all went tearing back the way we had come.

No one could call Sassoon anything but politically correct in modern terms. He was gay, a conscientious objector and a man of painful principles, but he called his autobiography *Memoirs of a Fox-Hunting Man* and chose to identify with 'this happy breed of men, this little world' that is hunting. He was a cousin by marriage and used to say that it was hunting that had given him the courage to stand up for what he believed in.

I have similar memories of my first hunt. I was ten years old when Dippy Parker, my best friend of the day, and I went out with the Puckeridge. It was a filthy wet day and as a wimpy London child I rather hoped we would postpone the outing till better weather. I had been a sickly child and, although I could ride, my mother hadn't let me hunt until now. Even then I think she was railroaded into it. There I was in my jodhpurs, hacking jacket and riding cap, all of a twitter with excitement. There is nothing more maddening than two small girls in a state of overexcitement. We got on our ponies and went to the meet nearby. I don't remember much of that as my stomach was full of butterflies but I suppose I spoke to people. Suddenly women pulled down their veils, men adjusted their gloves and hounds moved off. This bit I had seen before many times, but what came next? The rain trickled coldly down the back of my neck, my riding mac felt like an unhelpful burden, and I wasn't sure I wanted to be there – and then we were off.

If you haven't hunted, go out before you die: it is the most exhilarating, maddening, exciting, electric experience you will ever encounter. In all the times I hunted thereafter with all the packs, there was still that same electric feeling.

During the writing of this chapter I have asked a lot of people about the first time they went hunting: they all remembered and they all smiled at the memory. Whether like Johnny or his friend Guy (erstwhile Master of the Cheshire) they were led out on leading reins by puffing fathers who would rather have been on a horse; or like my friend Isabel who at ten remembers every ditch and every slither. Mr Christie my tailor, a quiet, gentle man who is slow to smile, became radiantly lit at the memory of himself as a small boy on a misty morning. People remember their children's first hunt, too. My friend Maggie described how she sat in her car fidgeting and fretting because she had people for dinner and the spuds weren't peeled and her daughter Fi wouldn't come back all day until she remembered that she hadn't either and now she has a grandchild who is just the same.

I met a girl called Alice who told me how at her pony club meet she had passed the field masters, passed the master, passed the hounds and finally there was a red brown blur and she had passed the fox! It is a sending-home offence to pass the master for all sorts of reasons,

I renamed my horse Nemesis

mainly to do with scent lines and his or her view of hounds, but I have never met anyone else who has passed the fox. I nearly became the first person to pass the master backwards on a Spanish horse of my mother's which she had bought from the famous *rejoneador* Angel Peralta. A *rejoneador* is a bullfighter who fights on horseback in the Portuguese manner. This animal was trained so that it would stand facing the 'gates of death' and then gallop backwards fast when the bull entered the ring to a fanfare of trumpets. Unfortunately it reacted the same way to any horns. I bailed out.

People love hunting for all sorts of reasons. Watching hounds work is one of them. After all, hounds have been bred to it for thousands of years. I have seen Michael Hedley, Master of the Border, standing dismounted by his hounds who were straining to go like kids out of school but all kept perfectly in check by his authority. They say 'the Master', the late great Duke of Beaufort, who hunted hounds four days a week, could check any of his hounds with just a twitch of an eyebrow. (The antis dug up his grave and took his head, just as they dug up John Peel's bones and scattered them.) None of this authority is exercised by violence or abuse, but by genuine bonding and affection.

Taking up the challenge again

Johnny O'Shea, legendary Huntsman of the Cheshire, summed it up in his Tipperary brogue: 'I loved the hounds and I loved the foxes. I was lucky to be paid for what I would have done anyway. I wasn't bred to hunt foxes as my hounds were so I just let them do it, and if I come back I'd do the same thing all over again. Sure I loved to pit my wits against that old fox.'

Some farmers, knowing the damage a fox can cause, are glad to see them killed, but by and large hunting people are much fonder of foxes than any other group I know. It is this dichotomy of the countryside, where death is a matter of course and has a different meaning than it has in towns, that causes a deal of misunderstanding. As a townie I have come to understand both perspectives and prefer that of the country. Death is not a thing to fear in the country but just an inevitable passing of the seasons.

People love hunting because they love to ride across country, especially when it is country they otherwise wouldn't be invited to ride over – although I don't see myself with the shire packs for all that my friend John says, 'A Monday with the Heythrop is a nice gentle day.' (When we were young barristers, his idea of gentle skiing was 'purple piste'. That may be the hardest for most people but not if you're into glacier skiing by helicopter or the 'black piste' of John's invention.)

From a quad to a horse in the morning

A horse shares the excitement with you too. Horses love hunting. In breeding stables the temperature of the brood mares rises at the sound of the hunt going by, whether they be thoroughbreds or shires. If you watch retired horses in a field they become most inspired and gallop down the field at the sound of the hunt. I used that analogy when I spoke to the twenty thousand people assembled for the Newcastle rally of the Countryside Alliance, comparing myself to an old horse who had heard the far-off sound of the horn, and everyone knew what I meant. If you have a sure-footed horse, preferably one that knows the country, it will do a lot of the work for you. I can remember the joy of finally having a pony that knew how to bend round poles. I really thought, aged eight, that it was me that had cracked it. If you get lost, a horse knows its way home and, apart from anything else, you feel more alive, more part of a team, more at one with the ancient traditions of the hunt if you do it on a horse.

Everyone loves the camaraderie. There is a real bonding between people who hunt. As Jorrocks says, 'Show me a man as hunts and I loves him.' I recently met an elderly couple who said that the best fun they had had in life was hunting. My darling Clive, who was a Field Master with the Bicester, would have agreed. The first time he took me back to his flat, he showed me his hunt buttons before anything else.

None of this has really explained to you why I want to return to hunting. My friend Annie Mallelieu, who reduced me and many others to tears at the first Hyde Park rally, said it best: 'This is our music and our song and the harmony of hounds giving tongue on a bright winter's morning is one of the best sounds in all the world.' Perhaps the threat of its removal has focused my mind to it again and made me remember what I miss.

Last year, when I went out on my quad bike with the Border, I thought for one fleeting moment as hounds moved off, 'I'm going hunting,' and maybe in that instant I fell in love again, for isn't it always love that makes us endure discomfort and vicissitude, makes us change our habits, rise at unseasonable hours, wear the clothes however unwieldy that our lover requires of us? It is why Mr Blair and his friends will not succeed in banning hunting for, in a Britain where there is so little love left for anything, 'this is our music and our song'. I want to see again hounds running across country giving tongue, to see them scenting about at the edges of a thicket, to feel the rain on my face and that bone-weary exhaustion that makes the bath at the end of a good hunting day the best in the world. I want some countryman with a weatherbeaten face and a coat his grandfather wore to come up to me again and say in the accents of his county, 'Zoom rider there, girl.'

So there you have it. Cynical, middle-aged, embattled, overweight and unfit, I am doing it for love.

INDEX

Picture credits

Christine Armstrong 133
J. & F.J. Baker 160, 161
BBC 99, 129, 136, 140, 147, 148
Camera Ways 56
G. L. Carlisle 55
Christies 8, 54, 70, 76
Corbis 36, 73, 86, 90, 102, 168, 174, 177, 179
Countryman's Weekly 23
English Heritage 105
Mary Evans 40, 84
Paul Felix 59, 62, 66, 158
Garden Matters 53
David Grant 114, 115
David Grewcock 51, 119, 173, 175
Illustrated London News 83
E. Jeffries 164
Carol Ann Johnson 24
David Jones 150
Kennel Club 25
Amanda Lockhart 154
Robin Matthews 6, 15,16, 17, 19, 21, 29, 30, 31, 32, 37, 38, 43, 48, 79, 93, 96, 97, 107, 108, 112, 113, 116, 121, 131, 132, 138, 141, 143, 152, 157, 159, 165, 167, 183, 184, 185, 187
Photobank 68
Scotland in Focus 126
Skyscan 64
Smiths of Herstmonceaux 60
Jim Stevens 123, 124
Simon Warner 46